KEEPING SAFE

This book was written to help parents and concerned adults to help children and young people develop skills which will protect them in many difficult or dangerous situations. The approach is practical, positive and based upon common sense. The book has been divided into two major sections. The first deals with potentially sexually abusive situations and how to deal with such situations should they arise. The second is about coping with bullies, drugs, alcohol abuse and AIDS.

Based on common sense and practical techniques, this book's message will not only reduce children's vulnerability, it will help them to be confident and keep safe.

About the Author

Michele Elliott is a teacher and educational psychologist with 20 years experience working with children and families. She is on the Advisory Councils of the NSPCC and ChildLine, and has chaired Home Office and World Health Organisation working groups on the subject of keeping children safe from sexual abuse. She is the author of two other books, *The Willow Street Kids* for young children and *Nicky's Safety Book* for under fives, as well a numerous articles. She is the founder and Director of the Kidscape Campaign for Children's Safety. She is married with two young sons.

Keeping Safe

Michele Elliott

with illustrations by Tony Wood

CORONET BOOKS
Hodder and Stoughton

Copyright © Michele Elliott 1985, 1986, 1988

First published privately as *Preventing Child Sexual Assault: a parents' guide to talking with children* 1984

A new, enlarged edition first published by Bedford Square Press as *Preventing Child Sexual Assault: a practical guide to talking with children* March 1985
Reprinted April 1985

Second edition September 1985
Reprinted with corrections February 1986

Third edition published as *Keeping Safe: a practical guide to talking with children* 1986

First New English Library Paperback edition 1988
Coronet edition 1992

Extract on physical and emotional abuse and neglect, and the Resource List Kidscape. Reproduced by kind permission of Kidscape.

British Library C.I.P.

Elliott, Michele
  Keeping safe.—3rd ed.
  1. Children. Sexual abuse by adults.
  Prevention
  I. Title II. Elliott, Michele.
  Preventing child sexual assault
  362.7'044

ISBN 0 340 579501

The right of Michele Elliott to be identified as the author of this work has been asserted by her in accordance with the Copyright, Designs and Patents Act 1988.

This book is sold subject to the condition that it shall not, by way of trade or otherwise, be lent, re-sold, hired out or otherwise circulated without the publisher's prior consent in any form of binding or cover other than that in which it is published and without a similar condition including this condition being imposed on the subsequent purchaser.

No part of this publication may be reproduced or transmitted in any form or by any means, electronic or mechanical, including photocopying, recording or any information storage or retrieval system, without either the prior permission in writing from the publisher or a licence, permitting restricted copying. In the United Kingdom such licences are issued by the Copyright Licensing Agency, 90 Tottenham Court Road, London W1P 9HE.

Printed and bound in Great Britain for Hodder and Stoughton Paperbacks, a division of Hodder and Stoughton Limited, Mill Road, Dunton Green, Sevenoaks, Kent TN13 2YA (Editorial Office: 47 Bedford Square, London WC1B 3DP) by Clays Ltd, St Ives plc.

This book is dedicated to Jan Stransky, Mark Providence-Perry, and to children everywhere in hope of the future

ACKNOWLEDGEMENTS

I gratefully acknowledge all the work to keep children safe which has been done by concerned people throughout the world. I especially thank for their kind help Wadad Haddad of the World Health Organisation; Sally Cooper of the Child Assault Prevention Project; Christina Smakowska, Librarian at the National Society for the Prevention of Cruelty to Children; Dr. Arnon Bentovim, Consultant Psychiatrist at Great Ormond Street Hospital for Sick Children; Chief Inspector Richard Lyttle of the Home Office Crime Prevention Centre; Dr. Peter Aggleton, Co-Director of Learning About AIDS; Patricia Crumpley, from the Tri-Valley Haven for Women; Ruth Hall, author; and Jacqueline Sallon, good friend and editor extraordinaire of Bedford Square Press; and grateful thanks are due as well to Kathy Gale, Senior Editor, and Broo Doherty, Junior Editor, at New English Library for all their help and advice.

Acknowledgement is made to the editor of *The Times Educational Supplement* for kind permission to reproduce certain material which appeared in my article entitled 'Caution' (*TES*, 18 April 1986).

I am very grateful, as well, to all my family and friends: Daphne Joiner, Heidi Amschwand, John Hadjipateras, Dee Dee Hadjipateras, John Ruddick, Linda Frost, and to my long-suffering husband Edward, and my two sons, Charles and James, for their continuing support, humour and excellent advice.

Special thanks to Claire Rayner for the time and effort she devotes to helping children and for her support.

CONTENTS

Preface ix
Kidscape xi
Foreword by Claire Rayner xiii

Introduction
Sexually abusive situations 1
Other dangers 11

Part 1: Child Sexual Abuse
1 Teaching Children How to Keep Safe 15
What parents can do 15
How to begin talking with children 17
What to do next 22
More suggestions for parents 33
Helping teenagers to protect themselves 37
How teachers and other adults can help 44
More suggestions for teachers and others 50
2 Dealing With Child Sexual Abuse 51
How to recognise the danger signs 51
What to do if you suspect abuse 57
What to do if an assault occurs 61

Part 2: Drugs, Alcohol, AIDS, Bullies and Other Dangers
3 Drugs, Solvent and Alcohol Abuse 75
What can parents do? 76
4 AIDS 83
AIDS at school 89
AIDS and child sexual abuse 89

5 Amusement Arcades	91
6 Pornographic Videos	93
7 Bullying	95
8 Other Tips for Safety	103
When to give independence	103
Tips on public places	104
Telephone tips	107
Tips on babysitters	112
Tips for teenagers when looking for part-time jobs	113
Conclusion	
9 Does prevention work?	119
10 Where to get help	124
Appendix I 'What if?' questions	135
Appendix II Questionnaires for young teenagers	147
Appendix III Questionnaires for older teenagers	157
Appendix IV Sources of information	171
Appendix V Signs of abuse	191

PREFACE

As a parent myself, I realise only too well how concerned we are to help children learn to deal with as many of the potential dangers in the world as possible. Hoping to help, I wrote the first version of this guide in 1984. It was designed to give parents a method of talking to children in a practical way without frightening them.

The original edition was entitled *Preventing Child Sexual Assault: A practical guide to talking with children*. At that time there were no books available for adults or children about the prevention of sexual assault, so the title was chosen to ensure that everyone knew exactly what we were talking about.

The concepts taught to children in the guide also covered ways to keep safe in other dangerous situations, from making emergency telephone calls in case of fire, to dealing with bullies and inappropriate approaches from strangers and known adults.

The tremendous feedback we received after publication of the first two editions led to the third edition, entitled *Keeping Safe*.

This, a further revised and expanded edition, is again in response to the demand for more information about how to answer children's questions about AIDS, how to help children deal with bullies, flashers or obscene telephone calls, safety factors for teenagers to consider when finding a job, information for parents about the issues of drug/solvent or alcohol abuse, how to help if a child has been abused and where to go for further information about all of these subjects. It also continues to include ways to talk with children and teenagers about keeping safe from possible sexual abuse.

Much has changed since the first three editions were published including the amount of information available to children and parents about keeping safe. For example, many children are now having personal safety taught to them through the Kidscape programme in schools; television and radio have introduced plays and short adverts about keeping safe; newspapers and magazines have countless articles about what to do to help children. As a result, parents may now find children and teenagers putting on an air of bravado, 'I know how to take care of myself,' or 'I've heard that before, I don't need to know any more'.

Don't be put off by this – learning these skills is an ongoing process. Just as we continue to teach road safety, so we must continue to teach personal safety. We are teaching children to use their judgement to keep themselves safe and this message needs to be reinforced in everyday life. If children say they know it all, reply that you are sure they know a lot and you are pleased that they do. But also emphasise that these kinds of skills and attitudes need to be practised and talked about until personal safety becomes a reflex action – a way of life.

KIDSCAPE

The Kidscape Campaign was formed following the two-year pilot project which involved parents, teachers and children in selected schools, play associations and other organisations throughout the United Kingdom. It was founded with the express aim of helping children to recognise and cope with potential dangers, from getting lost to dealing with bullies and strangers, and including the possibility of sexual assault.

The Kidscape programme has become known as Good Sense Defence. The programme teaches children through their parents and teachers to trust their own feelings in sensing dangerous situations; to differentiate between safe and unsafe forms of touching; to break rules when necessary in order to protect themselves; and always to seek adult help.

Although child-centred, Good Sense Defence depends upon and involves parents, teachers, youth workers, police – and all other concerned adults – for its complete integration into everyday life.

The first two of these programmes, for children under five and for five- to eleven-year-olds, have already been very successfully implemented into schools. The Teens programme is being piloted and will be available shortly.

We are continuing to work for children's safety and will gladly send you more information, should you like to contact us.

Kidscape
82 Brook Street
London W1 W1Y

FOREWORD by Claire Rayner

Back in the early nineteen fifties, first as a young nurse and then, later as a departmental Sister in a busy North London Paediatric Unit, I discovered a fact that was deeply distressing. A great many children and young people were suffering abuse of various kinds, and often sexual abuse, at the hands of the adults in their lives who were supposed to be caring for them. My first instinct then was to look after those children I met who had so suffered – after all, that was why I was a nurse; to offer care – and the second to be angry with the adults who perpetrated the abuse and to want to punish them, and the third was to tell everyone all about it so that children could be alerted and therefore could protect themselves.

I soon learned that of those three responses only one could really be applied: I could look after the children if they came into our wards. But I couldn't express my anger at the adults, for there was little proof of what the children told us happened to them (and too many in authority chose to regard them as liars) and I certainly couldn't publicise the matter. The general feeling around the hospital then, and I know the world at large, was that this was something you absolutely didn't talk about.

Once I became a medical journalist and started to deal with letters asking for help from the general public for their manifold problems, I then discovered that the problem of childhood abuse was even more widespread than I had realised *and always had been*. I had letters from women in their sixties and seventies and older still suffering psychological damage because of what had been done to them in childhood. Once again I tried to publicise the matter, but this time I met editorial resistance rather than the medical resistance of my nursing days. This was still something we didn't talk about...

Well, I persisted, as did other journalists and enlightened doctors, and gradually we have between us broken down the wall of silence. We can and do admit that this form of destructive behaviour goes on and that children need help to avoid it or resist it. And we also now realise that we must give such help if only so that the *chain* of abuse can be broken. Because tragically so often in the history of abusing adults is found the experience of childhood abuse. As the child received, so the adult gives...

Now I can see that one of my other wishes from the fifties is being granted – to give all the children the care they need. The best sort of care, which is not the sort that is applied from outside in the form of adult controls, adult watchfulness and adult anxiety (though these have their place) but in the form of solid information for the children themselves. The child who understands the risks the world carries and who is given strategies to deal with them is the best armoured child there can be. Innocence is never enhanced by ignorance, as people used to think. It is possible to arm children with all sorts of knowledge without damaging their intrinsic good heartedness and responsiveness to other good and caring people. That is the great gift that Michele Elliott offers children in this, her excellent book. With its help, our children will not only be safer; they will grow up to be genuinely caring and protective adults. And one day we must all hope there will be less and less need for my second wish – to punish the adults who perpetrate the abuse. Because they will not only be fewer, but we hope accessible to cure. Reading this book is necessary for all of us; children, abusing adults and would-be protective adults. We all have a lot to learn, and these pages can provide it.

Claire Rayner

INTRODUCTION

This book was written to help parents and other concerned adults to help children and young people develop skills which will protect them in many difficult or dangerous situations. The approach is practical, positive and based upon common sense. We have divided the book into two major sections. The first section is about keeping safe from potentially sexually abusive situations or abduction and how to deal with such situations should they arise. The second section is about coping with bullies, drugs, or questions about AIDS, as well as tips for young people about staying safe while working and for parents about what to look for when engaging a sitter, among other things.

SEXUALLY ABUSIVE SITUATIONS

Concern about child sexual abuse has grown in the last few years, and the number of reported cases has been steadily increasing throughout the world. The reports from adults about sexual abuse which happened to them as children have formed the basis of many statistical studies. The problem is not new, but what is new is public concern and the willingness of adults to listen and talk about their childhood secrets.

It is impossible to establish the exact number of adults who were sexually abused as children. From a recent MORI survey, it has been estimated that one in ten adults in the United Kingdom had at least one sexually abusive experience by the time they reached the age of sixteen. Other studies have placed the figure either higher or lower. These surveys usually ask about 'any sexually abusive experience' which can be a single incident or abuse that lasted over several years.

However, it is important not to overreact and think that all those reporting sexually abusive experiences were victims of rape or incest. Equally, we cannot dismiss the damage done by incidents of other kinds of sexual abuse to children. For example, one six-year-old girl who was flashed at started having nightmares, wetting the bed and becoming terrified whenever a man came near her. A four-year-old boy who was fondled by his uncle could not stand a male hugging him for over a year. Children subjected to prolonged abuse such as fondling, oral sex, indecent assault or incest can suffer even more severe consequences. Some are disturbed for life, unable to form lasting relationships, becoming drug addicts, prostitutes or committing suicide to escape from the pain. Others manage to integrate the abuse into their life experiences and carry on without outwardly showing the effects. (See Appendix 5.)

But the damage it does its victims makes sexual abuse a cause for great concern. More and more treatment programmes are being developed to help the victims and their families. Adult survivors of sexual abuse are setting up self-help groups and telephone counselling services are becoming more widely available. Some progress is also being made to help those who abuse.

Parents are also becoming more aware of the need to help children recognise potentially abusive situations, yet many feel unsure about discussing the subject with their offspring. Instead they try to supervise their children as much as possible, and rely uneasily on the good intentions of others.

This is not enough. Unfortunately, the vast majority of sexual abuse of children is committed by someone the child knows: a neighbour, friend, babysitter or family member. In over seventy-five per cent of the cases of sexual abuse reported to the police, the abuser was known to the child. Therefore, telling children to beware only of strangers still leaves them vulnerable to the approaches of someone they know.

It is like teaching them to cross the road and to watch out just for red cars.

What is child sexual abuse?

There are many definitions of child sexual abuse. It is difficult to find one which satisfies everyone. Perhaps the most simple and straightforward definition is:

Child sexual abuse is any sexual exploitation of a child under the age of sixteen for the sexual pleasure, gratification or profit of an adult or significantly older person.

This ranges from obscene telephone calls, indecent exposure and voyeurism, such as spying on a child undressing, to fondling, taking pornographic pictures, intercourse or attempted intercourse, buggery, rape, incest or involving children in prostitution. It may be a single incident or events which occur over a number of years.

Another definition of child sexual abuse, widely accepted by experts and often quoted, comes from C. Henry

Kempe the recognised authority in this field:

> Child sexual abuse is the involvement of developmentally immature children and adolescents in sexual activities they do not truly comprehend to which they are unable to give informed consent or that violate the social taboos of family roles.

But whatever the definition of child sexual abuse, it is generally agreed that children are naturally affectionate and seek the attention of adults, and when an adult or anyone significantly older uses children as sexual objects or partners, it is inappropriate and irresponsible behaviour.

What about sexual play between children?

It is important when defining sexual abuse to exempt the normal play of children which often includes exploring their own bodies and those of other children. When the children are within the same age range and are playing doctors and nurses, this is a normal, healthy part of growing up. It may feel good and be sensual, but it is neither sexual in an adult sense, nor abuse.

This play becomes abusive if there is a large age gap between the children, such as a thirteen-year-old 'playing with' a four-year-old, or if a child is being *forced* to participate.

There are times when a child who has been abused may attempt to act out the abuse on another child. In this case, the level of sexual knowledge of the child who initiates the incident is most often totally inappropriate to his or her age, such as a three-year-old accurately trying to enact oral sex on another child. The child who is 'abusing' is in reality a victim who should be referred for help.

There is also growing concern about the possibility of young children imitating what they may have seen on a pornograhic video (see page 93). At this point we cannot discount the possibility that children may try out what they see. However, we have no evidence at this time to support the idea that children who see these videos have understood enough to learn how to try out sexual activities with other children. What we are finding is that young children who react in a sexually inappropriate way which appears abusive, have themselves been abused.

What about children being interested in adults' bodies?

Many parents have recounted the occasions when a son or daughter has been fascinated with the mother's breasts, the father's penis or some other part of their bodies. Sometimes the child wants to touch or look at various parts of the body and adults are embarrassed or even shocked. One father was particularly worried that it might be misinterpreted as sexual abuse because his three-year-old daughter wanted to touch his penis in the bath.

Children are quite often interested in adult bodies. Again it is a natural part of growing up. This kind of curiousity should not be threatening to adults, though in the current climate, it is an understakable worry. As long as the child is instigating the questions or the touching in a way appropriate to the child's age and it is not being kept a secret, it is not abuse.

If, however, a child tries to enact something totally inappropriate, you should be concerned about where the child learned the behaviour. For example, in one case a five-year-old girl began acting seductively in a very adult manner and attempted to get her parent to fondle her. The child had been abused by a babysitter, and since in this case it had felt good, she tried to get her parent to do the same thing. Clearly, this child's behaviour was cause for concern. The parent had to set limits (see page 38) by saying no to the child's request and had to seek help to find out what had happened to the child.

But we should not be concerned about children's natural sensual and sexual development which includes looking at their own and other people's bodies. The more open and honest we can be with them when they ask questions, the easier it will be to help them develop ways to keep safe.

Who are the offenders?

Just as there are no definitions of child sexual abuse which satisfy everyone, neither is there one simple and satisfactory explanation about who are the offenders. Most of the information known about child abusers comes from studies done in prisons. Since relatively few offenders are apprehended, convicted and sent to prison, our knowledge of them is limited.

From records kept of offences, it is known that approximately ninety-five per cent of reported offenders are men and this statistic has been consistent in studies throughout the world. (This should not be misinterpreted, however, to say that most men molest children.)

Little is known about women offenders, except that at this time there are very few reported cases. In surveys of adults talking about child sexual abuse, women are rarely mentioned as the perpetrators. However, in cases which are coming to light, the trauma for the victim is just as great regardless of the sex of the offender.

There are many ways to describe child abusers. Nicholas Groth, an expert in treating offenders, has classified them into two main categories:

- **Paedophiles**

    People who have always been sexually attracted to children and who are not generally interested in sex with adults are commonly called paedophiles. Their interest in children often began when they were very young teenagers and it is extremely difficult to change their behaviour. Many paedophiles believe that it is a child's right to have sex with adults and say that they love children and would not harm them.

Groth has found that these offenders are usually attracted to little boys. They will go out of their way to become friends with a child and plan the 'seduction' over a long period of time. If the child says no, they will often move on to another child. They also tend to discard a child when the child begins to show signs of physical maturity. Therefore paedophiles are often Peter Pan-type characters, actually not wanting to grow up or be involved with adults. Children are a reflection of their own narcissism.

- **Regressed Child Molesters**

The regressed child molester is usually married or involved in a relationship. They either have children of their own or have stepchildren, and these children become their primary victims.

Most regressed child molesters have or have had a sexual relationship with another adult. However, during times of stress, they cannot cope with this adult relationship and turn to children for unconditional love, nurturance and sex. Once children are caught in this kind of trap, where the offender has power over every aspect of their lives, it is sometimes impossible to escape.

Most of the victims of the regressed molesters are girls and they are not discarded on reaching puberty. In fact, since the men are looking for substitute wives, adolescent girls continue to be at risk from the abuse which often started when they were quite young.

We know that offenders have abused babies as young as a month old and children right up to the age of sixteen. We also recognise that girls and boys are almost equally at risk. Some offenders abuse girls and boys, some prefer one sex.

Child molesters come from every class, profession, racial and religious background. Some studies have shown that a high percentage of offenders were themselves physically or sexually abused as children. What is not clear is why so many children who were abused do *not* become offenders. Equally, why do some men become child molesters, though they were not abused as children? More information is needed about offenders so that effective treatment programmes can be instigated in the hope of preventing more children from becoming victims.

There are several particularly disturbing factors in trying to prevent child sexual abuse. One factor is that child molesters, such as paedophiles, tend to gravitate towards places, professions and activities which put them into direct contact with children. They usually look and act normally and often hold responsible jobs. They sometimes attach themselves to families, offer to babysit and to take the children out.

Unfortunately this means that children can and do come into contact with people who may try to abuse them. It also means that children may not be believed because the abuser 'is such a nice person that it must be the child who is lying'.

Another factor is how difficult it is to stop the confirmed child abuser. Power is often the motivating force behind the actions of child sexual abusers and in many ways the offence is not about sex. But once the offender has begun abusing children, it quickly becomes an addictive tendency. It becomes a source of gratification and the abuser is not inclined to stop. This is why it is so difficult to treat sexual abusers and why they remain a threat to children. Without motivation people do not change their behaviour. Even if they are caught, the risk of reoffending appears to be very high.

Another concern is that, as several studies show, many victims are created by offenders. One long-term American study by Gene Abel from the New York Institute of Psychiatric Medicine shows that child molesters average seventy-three victims before they are caught. Offenders are usually able to avoid detection because they become expert at hiding their deviant behaviour from their families, friends and colleagues and because children are easily coerced into silence by adult authority.

Until we can apprehend the offenders and effectively change their behaviour, children will continue to be at risk. We must work to change not only the abusers but society's attitudes which encourage their activities. Realistically this will take years, if not centuries. In the meantime, however, we cannot leave children vulnerable to the greater cunning and manipulative powers of these people.

We have to teach children to tell and seek help – it is the only effective method of prevention currently available.

(For more detailed information about offenders, see pages 25–8).

The need for preventive techniques

Fortunately, most children will not become victims of sexual abuse, just as most children will not be victims of drowning or traffic accidents. However, in the same way that parents teach children from the time that they are very young that there are ways to stay safe from dangers in the world, children can be taught practical ways to keep safe from abuse. Children take the messages in their stride and enjoy learning about personal safety. This can easily be done in a manner which is neither frightening nor unrealistic.

Since the majority of sexual offences against children are committed by someone known to the child, it is apparent that children must be taught how to prevent this kind of abuse by anyone, not just strangers. It is important to talk with children because lack of information is one of the main reasons why children are vulnerable to abuse. By teaching children to avoid dangerous situations, to recognise inappropriate touching, to say no when anyone tries to do something which makes them frightened or confused, to refuse to keep secrets, and to seek adult help, parents can begin to prevent sexual abuse.

All children need this kind of protection. Sexual abuse of children can occur within every neighbourhood, every class and every racial background. There are also numerous reports of abuse of children in care or in foster homes and of physically and mentally handicapped children.

The message of prevention is the same for all children and the ideas in this book can be adapted according to the individual child, his or her level of understanding, age, cultural background or circumstances.

Children cannot be expected to take full responsibility for keeping themselves safe. It is the responsibility of all adults, especially parents and teachers. That is why a prevention programme which makes personal safety a normal part of every-day life is essential.

Children who know preventive techniques are not only less at risk because they are informed, but they are also more confident about themselves. Parents and teachers who can talk with children in a supportive, loving atmosphere and help them learn ways to stay safe are giving children a basis for life-long self-protection.

Although it is unrealistic to think that the problem of child sexual abuse can be eliminated entirely, or that all children can be kept safe, adults can recognise the problem and learn to teach children about it. With our help, children can be taught to use and trust their own judgement to protect themselves and become more safe, aware and confident.

OTHER DANGERS

There are, of course, many other potential dangers facing children and their parents. It is important for children to learn strategies for coping with these dangers in order to be able to keep safe, but also because teaching them to trust their feelings and express their concerns in other issues gives them general skills for keeping safe. If, for example, children are being bullied, giving them support and strategies will encourage them to approach adults for help when even more serious concerns arise. By helping them to understand what could happen if they take drugs or drink, we might give them the strength to say no when confronted with a dilemma. By answering their questions about AIDS, we could save their lives. Most children will face at least one of the dangers talked about in this book. Perhaps the strategies which we teach them, along with our support and example, might make a difference.

In the second section of the book we thus deal with ideas and strategies for keeping safe on issues as diverse as drugs, solvent and alcohol abuse; AIDS; bullying and gambling; and give general tips on using telephones, lifts and stairways, public toilets, babysitters, and on teenagers in part-time work.

Whether we are dealing with bullies at school, with teenagers drinking, or with children being abused, it is important to have methods for prevention, protection and, if necessary, cure. We hope this volume will provide practical ways of achieving all three.

Michele Elliott, 1988

Part 1: Child Sexual Abuse

1 TEACHING CHILDREN HOW TO KEEP SAFE

WHAT PARENTS CAN DO

Encouraging children to express their feelings

Parents want to help their children grow into happy and confident adults. A child's ability or inclination to trust, to feel good about achievements, to share, and to be confident are learned from parents and other people with whom the child comes into contact.

These experiences form the basis for children learning strategies for keeping safe. This learning process starts from the time they are very young. For example, the best way for a child to learn to differentiate between furtive, false affection and normal, everyday affection is to experience open, loving hugs and kisses and positive relationships with adults.

But even this normal, healthy affection is becoming a problem for some people in the light of concern about sexual abuse. Fathers and other men are starting to feel uneasy about hugging or touching children, lest their affection be wrongly interpreted. One father said he was now worried when his children piled into bed for an early morning cuddle. Another felt himself holding back when his son wanted a goodnight kiss.

This kind of attitude makes men uncomfortable and harms children. Children need affection – from men and women.

Frederick II, a thirteenth century king, once conducted an experiment in which he told foster mothers and nurses to feed and bathe the babies in their care, but not to speak to them or cuddle them. According to the Medieval writer Salimbene, Frederick wanted to find out what kind of speech and manner the children would have without ever being taught. The experiment ended tragically, as all the babies died!

Not all children who are deprived of love die, but they do need a strong foundation of love for building their confidence and the ability to cope. Children thrive on our cuddles and we certainly need theirs. So when children seek affection and it is given freely and openly, no one should feel uneasy.

By extending this openness to communication between parents and children, we can encourage children to tell us if anything frightening or untoward happens to them so we can help. But to do this we must allow and, indeed, encourage children to express their feelings.

Children are often made to believe that they are not allowed to have feelings or that their feelings are unimportant. For example, if Brian comes home with a skinned, bleeding knee and our response is, 'For goodness sake, Brian, stop crying. It doesn't hurt!', who is Brian to believe – his own feelings or our message? Will Brian then tell us when something else happens or will he expect us to say, 'don't be so silly!'? The same applies if children dislike someone and are told that 'it is not polite to say no'. What will they do if someone asks them to get into a car, to play a secret game or to try drugs?

What about being forced to kiss people goodbye or endure unwanted tickling? We cannot teach children to trust their feelings and tell us if they feel unsafe, while at the same time make them suppress those very feelings.

Encouraging children to trust and to express their feelings, and believing them when they do, is the basis of learning any strategies for keeping safe, whether the problem is bullies, possible sexual abuse or drugs.

HOW TO BEGIN TALKING WITH CHILDREN

There are several ways to begin a conversation with children about keeping safe. Two simple and direct methods which have worked most successfully are starting off by talking about personal safety rights; or about touching which feels good, safe or comfortable and touching which feels bad, unsafe, or is secretive.

Discuss the right to be safe

Explain to children that everyone has rights which

should not be taken away from them. Start with simple ideas such as the right to breathe, eat, sleep, play or go to the toilet. Ask children what would happen if the right to eat was taken away from them. Would that create problems? What if they were not allowed to go to the toilet?

Children should be encouraged to think about what would happen to start them using their own judgement. Ask them to think of ways to get their rights back. One child said that if she were not allowed to eat, she would collect berries. Another said that he would go on strike and picket his house with a sign saying 'unfair to children'.

After children clearly understand this concept, use it to discuss the right to be safe. Ask them when they feel safe, and ask them to give specific examples such as 'when my parents tuck me into bed with a goodnight kiss'

or 'when playing with my friends' or 'when reading a story with Mummy'. One five-year-old said that being safe was 'not having to stay with the lions in the zoo'. Explain that sometimes people try to take away the rights of others, including the right to be safe.

Emphasise to children that they should say no and get help when someone tries to take away their rights and that you will support them in this. Make sure that children understand that the right to be safe includes the right to say what happens to their own bodies. (See the later suggestions about saying no and talking with children about their bodies.)

Discuss safe touches and unsafe touches

Another approach is to begin with an explanation of touching which feels safe or unsafe which the child may refer to as good or bad touches. You can introduce this by talking about how nice a hug or kiss can be and by asking children how they would show someone they love them (without giving a tangible gift such as a puppy or toy). One child said he would give someone he loved 1,000 hugs and kisses every day. If you have a pet, ask children what kind of touches the pet likes or dislikes. Then ask what kind of touches children like or dislike. Children may say they like soft hugs and big kisses. They often mention that tickling is fun, but not too much or too long. Many children relate that they hate being patted on the head.

Explain that children have the right to say no, even to someone they love, if they do not like a touch or a kiss. This means that children should not be forced to be affectionate with anyone, even their own parents.

Parents can help their children politely to refuse kisses or hugs that make them uncomfortable, even in an everyday situation. If necessary, explain that your child is going through a 'shy stage' or be totally honest and say that your child is learning to say no to requests that make him or her uncomfortable. If we force children to be affectionate because we as adults are embarrassed if they are not, we are not helping them. Children must begin to trust their own feelings and judgement if they are to learn to keep themselves safe.

This also means that children will have to learn that there are times when the rules of being polite do not apply and it might be necessary to break them.

There are many different cultural customs about hugging, kissing and touching. There is no reason for these to change. However, in any culture it is inappropriate for an adult to seek contact with children as a result of his or her own sexual needs or if the adult is seeking to be sexually stimulated by the contact.

Teach children to say no

Instead of teaching children to listen to and obey all adults without question, tell them that they have your permission and support to say no to protect themselves. Help them to practise saying no in an assertive way because it is very difficult for most children to say no to an adult.

In the classroom or at home, adults can help children to learn to say no by asking if it is easy to say no to someone older. Children usually say that it is difficult to refuse an adult's request or command. Explain that you are going to help them practise saying no. This will enable them to say no if someone asks them to do anything which makes them confused or uncomfortable.

Start with questions children can easily say no to such as:

Adult: 'Do you like cheese?'
Child: 'No.'
Adult: 'Wouldn't you like a cheese sandwich?'
Child: 'No.' (Said from a distance.)

Proceed to questions requiring caution:

Adult: 'Can you tell me how to get to the cinema?'
Child: 'No.'

Most adults do not ask children for directions, so it is safer to tell children not to get involved. Tell children that they should not enter into conversation, nor give reasons for not talking. If an adult comes close to the child, he or she should move quickly away and say nothing.

Children can offer suggestions and the idea of saying no in an assertive way can be learned in a safe environment. Practising will help to make saying no automatic in a potentially dangerous situation. Along with not keeping secrets and knowing about bad touching, saying no can be an especially effective deterrent against the non-violent offender who is known to the child. One man who had molested three of his four children was asked why he did not abuse the fourth. 'She said "no"', was his answer.

However, it is not always possible for a child to say no because of fear or the threat of violence. It may be necessary for the child to comply with the adult's demand and then seek help by telling. When teaching children to say no, they should be told that there may be times when they cannot and that you will understand and support them. The most important message is that you want them to be safe.

WHAT TO DO NEXT

Talk to children about their bodies

Explain to children that their bodies are their own and that no one should touch them in a way which makes them confused or uncomfortable. Help them understand that this means their whole body from the top of their head to their toes, as well as the private parts of their bodies. Teach children the correct names of their private parts. However, if this makes you uncomfortable, another explanation is 'those parts covered by your bathing suit'. (Even if you do teach your children the correct names, they usually learn a variety of terms at school. My children went to school with penises and came home with willies!)

The terms you use are not nearly as important as teaching children that they have the right to control what happens to their bodies. There is no need to give children too much information, which could frighten them. But even young children have a strong sense of their own identity and what they like and dislike.

Talk about safe secrets versus unsafe secrets

Since offenders who are known to children often depend upon children's willingness to keep secrets, it is extremely effective to teach children, even very young ones, to say no to this request.

In some families, children are taught to keep surprises,

but never to keep secrets. Another method is to teach children the difference between safe or unsafe secrets. Ask children to suggest a safe secret. They will probably mention a birthday present, or surprise party or mummy having another baby. See if they can describe an unsafe secret. Some examples that children have offered are: 'Daddy and Mummy are fighting', 'knowing your friend has taken something from a shop', or 'a bully who takes away your money and you are too scared to tell'.

When children understand the difference between safe and unsafe secrets, they are ready to be taught that no one should ask them to keep touching a secret. This applies to all touching, even if it feels good. Tell children that they should always tell a trusted adult if anyone asks them to keep such a secret. Help children make a list of people they feel they can talk to if they have a problem, or let them make a list by themselves.

One difficulty in dealing with child sexual abuse is that sometimes the victims experience physical pleasure. This often compounds the confusion and makes the children feel that they are accomplices and that their bodies have betrayed them. An added problem may be that the abuser is also the only person from whom the child is receiving any type of affection, however inappropriate. This is particularly true if the abuser is a member of the child's family. By telling children that no touches, hugs or kisses should be kept secret, you are helping them to define the boundaries and giving them permission to seek adult help. Children may feel responsible or even guilty about what has happened and you must try to give them a way of telling in order to help to relieve that burden.

Encourage children to tell

Assure your children that no matter what happens you will not be angry with them and that you want them to tell you of any incident. Explain the difference between telling tales to get someone into trouble and getting help when someone is threatening their safety. Ask children to give examples of telling tales, such as running to the teacher because another child is using the swings when they want to swing. Then talk about dangerous situations in which a child should get help. One child described a time when his bicycle had been taken from him and the teenager threatened him with a beating if he told anyone.

Explain to children that even if they break a home or school rule which leads to them getting into difficulty, you still want to know and you will not blame them. An eleven-year-old girl broke the family rule about going through the park to get home after school. A man forced her into the bushes and indecently assaulted her. He told her he would find her and kill her if she told someone. She eventually told her parents, who immediately comforted her and assured her that it was the offender who was guilty, not her. They did not say, 'See what happens when you don't listen?' The child knew she should not have gone across the park, but to have made her feel guilty would not have been helpful.

By giving your children the assurance that you will support them, no matter what circumstances preceded the incident, you will help them to cope better with an assault, should it occur. If you do not give this kind of assurance and mean it, your children will not tell you for fear that you will be angry with them.

Since children often feel that adults do not believe them, encourage children to keep telling until someone does and the children get help.

Caution about telling

One freely available leaflet advises parents to tell their children to say to the offender, 'I'm going to tell!' This is not wise because it could lead to real physical harm. It is one thing to say no when possible, quite another to threaten an offender with disclosure. Be certain that you explain to children and to young people not to tell the offender that they will tell, but to get away first no matter what they have to promise. They can then wait until they feel more safe to talk.

Talk about presents versus bribes

Child molesters, both adults known to children and strangers, often offer children bribes in exchange for sexual favours. Children should be taught what bribes are and what those who offer bribes seek to accomplish.

Ask children to give you examples of gifts, such as birthday or holiday presents given to celebrate a happy occasion. These gifts may be kept as a surprise secret before they are given, but are not kept a secret when they are received. Explain that gifts and bribes are different. The message that children need to learn is that gifts are given freely with no conditions and that bribes are given to make them do something they do not want to do.

One child said that his teacher 'bribed' him with gold stars to do his maths, which he didn't want to do. The child definitely understood the concept of bribery, but it is the secretive, furtive element of 'don't tell anyone and I'll give you some sweets' which should be emphasised.

Talk about tricks

Explain to children that some people, both known adults and strangers, might try to trick them by offering them a present, money, sweets or a trip to the zoo or cinema to do something they don't like. Tell them that if that happens they should say something like, 'I must ask my Mum, Dad or my teacher', and get away quickly to seek help.

A common trick used by molesters is, 'Your Mum is sick and asked me to take you to her'. One suggestion that many parents have used is to have a code word, known only to the parents and children. If you must send someone to collect children in an emergency, the person sent would use the agreed code.

Tell children that you want to be told if anyone offers them a bribe or tries to trick them.

Do not define people as good or bad

If children think only bad people hurt them, they will not be prepared for the person who approaches them in a manner which gains their trust. By teaching them the danger signs, you will be protecting them far better than by telling them to watch out for 'bad' people. One method of relating this is to explain that people have good and bad in them and sometimes even good people do things we do not like.

The mother of a ten-year-old boy said that her son had been taught to say no to strangers and was confident that he could take care of himself. One afternoon after school when the boy was alone, a man wearing a business suit and carrying a briefcase knocked on the door. The boy opened the door, using the safety chain. The man claimed that he was taking his pregnant wife to the hospital, their car had broken down and he had to telephone for an ambulance. The boy offered to telephone for him, but the man insisted that this was an emergency and there was no time to spare. The boy let him in and was sexually assaulted. His mother said that her son told her afterwards that the man had not seemed to be a 'bad person' because he was dressed 'like Daddy and did not look like a stranger'.

Most children do not understand the concept of 'stranger'. When asked to describe strangers, children will say they are dirty, weird, ugly, smelly and suspicious. Anyone who fits a child's concept of 'nice' is not a stranger. Even if they understand that strangers are people you do not know, children quickly take people out of this category.

It is important to emphasise that they should get away if anyone tries to do something which makes them frightened or confused. Tell children that if anyone approaches them and tries to talk to them when they are on their own, they should pretend not to hear and walk away, saying nothing. It is better to do that and perhaps hurt someone's feelings than to take a chance and get hurt oneself.

Answer children's questions

When children are concerned about television programmes, nightmares, newspaper reports or tragedies, answer their questions carefully and sensitively without dismissing their feelings or denying the reality of the situation. This helps children to trust their own feelings and judgement and is better than telling them not to worry. Children will not share their feelings if they are not taken seriously.

However, there is no need to frighten children with too much information. Understand what children are really asking and give them the facts gradually until they are satisfied with the answer. For example, one five-year-old girl asked her mother what rape was because she heard the word on television. The mother's response was to find out what her daughter thought it was and to proceed from there. In this case the explanation that it meant someone touching her private parts in a way she did not like was all that was needed. If an older child had asked the same question, he or she would probably need more information and a fuller explanation. Explaining instead of avoiding is the important message so that children will feel confident in asking questions because they will know that they will receive honest answers.

Believe your children

Children rarely lie about sexual abuse which has occurred: they do not have the language or experience. They may, however, later deny that abuse took place to protect someone they love or because they are afraid. Children may also get the details confused because of the traumatic nature of what has happened. When dealing with children, question gently but do not interrogate.

Ask for the reasons when children do not want to go to someone's house or do not like a babysitter, or when their behaviour patterns change dramatically (see pages 51–7). Gently draw out more information about comments such as 'I don't like the way John teases me' or 'The man at the shop acts funny'. Although these comments usually indicate something harmless, parents must learn to be sensitive to what their children are trying to say. One child told her mother that her uncle teased her and she didn't like it. The mother responded that everyone gets teased growing up and she would have to get used to it. The child was very upset, but did not say anything else. Several months later, the girl was diagnosed as having gonorrhoea of the throat. Her uncle called it teasing and she was too young to know better.

Create an atmosphere of trust in which children know they will be listened to and believed. They will then be encouraged to share their concerns and thus potentially harmful situations can be avoided.

Play 'what if?' games

Children often ask 'what would happen if . . . ?' type questions, which parents can turn into a fun learning game. Instead of answering immediately, ask your children what they think would happen. This gives them a chance to test their ideas and judgement about the world. Parents can initiate questions as well, but should be careful not to ask questions that may frighten children.

With young children it might be better to start with something like 'What would you do if a monkey came to the door?' Then, if the child is interested, ask other questions which are appropriate to his or her age. (Since the monkey is a stranger, by the way, the child should not let it in!) This can lead to a discussion of who would be let in: what if someone was dressed like Daddy or said Mummy was ill, etc. Questions like 'What if someone you know tries to touch you in a way you do not like?' should be included when the child is ready.

Playing 'what if?' games, either at home or in school, is a good way for children to learn many concepts. You can start with a variety of situations not related to assaults. For example:

Adult: 'What if you saw smoke coming from your neighbour's house?'
Child: 'I would ring the fire brigade.'
Adult: 'How would you do that? Show me.'

This would be a good way to teach a child about making 999 calls. (See pages 107–9.) Examples of preventive 'what if?' games might be:

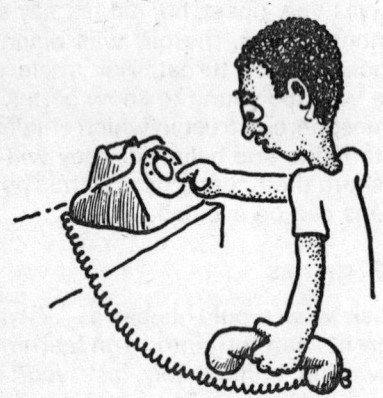

Adult: 'What if someone said he or she was a friend of Daddy's and asked you to go with him or her to a house?'
Child: 'I would not go and would run away if anyone got too close. I would tell a grown-up what had happened.'

When the children are prepared for the more sensitive questions, ask:

Adult: 'What if a babysitter or relative you liked asked

you to play secret games, and offered to let you stay up late (or give you a present or money, etc.)?'
Child: 'I would say that I am not allowed to keep secrets.'
Adult: 'What if the person insisted?'
Child: 'I would say no. When it was safe, I would tell.'
Adult: 'Well done!

One mother told me how she got off a bus with her baby and was turning around to collect her other child, when the bus left. Eventually she was reunited with the child, but after much anxiety and tears all round.

So, another 'what if?' question might be:

Adult: 'What would you do if we were on a bus or tube and somehow I got off and you did not?'
Child: 'I would get off and meet you at the very next bus stop. I would get off at the next underground station and stay on the platform and tell the station manager what had happened.'
Adult: 'What would you do if you accidentally got off at a stop before me?'
Child: 'I would stay there and wait for you to come and collect me.'

Alternatively, you may want to give different instructions, such as stay on the bus and tell the conductor what has happened. What you decide will depend upon the age of your children and the locality in which you usually travel.

Adult: 'What would you do if you were lost?'
Child: 'I would stay at the place I was and wait for you to find me. I would tell the person in charge of the store what had happened, but not leave or go outside.'
The store is probably a safe place to wait.

The common message here is for the child to wait for the adult to collect them, rather than for the child to set out in search of the adult.

When travelling, shopping or taking children to a busy place, it is important to have a plan about what to do and where to meet should you become separated. This will give everyone a strategy and hopefully result in a quick reunion.

One example when shopping might be:

Adult: 'If we get lost from each other, we will meet at the water fountain.'

Be sure to actually show the meeting place to the children so that they are not confused. Emphasise that they should not go outside the shop or area. These kind of instructions are becoming more necessary as we take children to theme parks and other places where we and they are not familiar with the locality.

Always try to praise ideas children have about keeping themselves safe. This encourages them to continue to think creatively. Other suggested topics for 'what if?' games might be what to do:

- if you lost your way
- if you saw a road accident
- if a stranger tried to talk to you when you were on your own
- if you went to the shop to buy bread, but the shop had run out
- if you were home alone and someone came to the door (Children should never be left home alone, but they need to know what to do should this occur.)

Have children make up 'what if?' questions for each other and for you (see pages 139–45 for additional ideas of 'what if?' questions).

Give children permission to break rules

If children find themselves in a difficult situation, they may not be able to deal with it because they feel restrained by all the everyday rules they have been taught. In teaching children to keep themselves safe, we must tell them that there are exceptions to every rule.

For example, children are taught to be polite, not to lie, not to tell tales, and certainly not to resist adults. Yet to keep themselves safe children may need to break one or more of these rules. Parents should discuss this with their children (by using the 'what if?' game) and give them permission to make exceptions.

The most important message you can teach children is that they have the right to use any method to keep themselves safe in a potentially dangerous situation. Again, using language appropriate to their age, tell children it is all right not to answer the door, to say no to someone they love, to yell, run, bite, kick, lie, break a window, etc. Remind them that the object is always to run, get away and seek adult help. Give them your permission to break all rules to protect themselves and tell them you will support them.

The father of six-year-old Adam who was abducted and murdered said:

> 'Adam was a model child, he never even went to the park by himself. He never disobeyed, never. I taught him to listen to adults, to respect his elders and to be a little gentleman. I never taught him how to scream. He might be alive if he had screamed.'

MORE SUGGESTIONS FOR PARENTS

- Teach children their full names, addresses and telephone numbers. If children are lost, they will know how to contact you. This is also helpful should they need to make an emergency telephone call.

- Do *not* teach children to answer the telephone by repeating their name or telephone number.

- Help children practise making an emergency telephone call. (See page 108.)

- Evaluate children's regular walking routes and playing places. This will help children to know the best ways to get home and where it is safest to play. Children should avoid isolated play places and paths, and being out at night alone.

- Do not put names on the outside of children's clothes or books. This gives an adult who is intending to harm a child advantage. Children might be confused if someone they do not know suddenly said hello using their name. It makes them think that the stranger knows them.

- Watch for negative reactions to people and explore suspicious comments children may make about adults, older children or teenagers, babysitters, etc. Most of the time there will be a harmless reason, such as the child-minder made the child take a nap when the child did not want to. However, there could be other reasons. One child said she hated the neighbour's hamster and did not want to go there any more. The parents learned eventually that the neighbour had been interfering with her and she did not know how to talk about what was happening.

- Help children to establish a network of trusted adults to whom they can turn for help.

- Teach basic techniques such as never go with a stranger, always stay two arm lengths from a stranger (demonstrate that it is difficult to grab someone from that distance), never answer the door when at home alone or admit over the telephone to being alone. Practise telephone answers such as 'My mother is in the bath. If you will leave your number, she will ring you back'.

- In the first few seconds of an attack, a reactive child might have the advantage of surprise because the attacker is expecting a child to be passive and scared. Since getting away is the object, a child can surprise an attacker and run for help: immediate, noisy and active resistance is the key. Even very young children can be taught to yell loudly and run. An older child can be taught to scream, kick the attacker's knee with the heel of his or her foot, scrape down the attacker's inside calf in the same motion, stamp as hard as possible on the attacker's foot, and run to get away. Another technique for the older child is to bring his or her elbow into the attacker's stomach or groin and run. Remember that we are talking about a very dangerous situation in which it is possible that the child will be badly hurt and the only chance is to get away. The goal is to startle or hurt the attacker enough to run away.

- Tell children never to chase an attacker. Tell them to leave that to the police or other adults.

- Play games involving observation skills such as looking at objects on a tray for ten seconds and recalling them from memory. Ask a member of the family to come into the room for ten seconds, then leave. Try to recall as many details as possible about him or her. While travelling in the car, see who can call out registration numbers on red cars, etc. These observation skills are useful in everyday life, but may also be vital in describing what happened or what someone looked like, if a child is attacked.

- Tell children not to react to flashers. Many children report being flashed at on the underground, near playgroups, in parks and at bus stops. It can be quite terrifying and has led to nightmares and other problems. Explain that the person doing this is looking for a reaction, even if it is laughter or rude comments. The very best thing to do is not to look, get away from the situation as soon as possible and tell an adult immediately.

    One eleven-year-old girl was standing at her bus stop when a man came up to her and flashed. She had the presence of mind to walk away quickly into a shop, but she got a good description of the man and the police were able to act on her information. She later reported that she had not been frightened and did not panic because she knew what to do.

    Again, giving children strategies is far better than making them fearful.

- Check with other parents concerning your babysitter's reliability and behaviour (see pages 112–13).

- If your child has a nightmare and is afraid to go back to sleep, turn on the light and search the room with him or her. This will comfort the child far more than saying there is nothing there. It will also assure your child that you listen and believe what he or she says and that you are prepared to intervene actively to help. This kind of listening could be quite important for future communication.

However, make sure that this is comforting to your child and that he or she doesn't end up thinking you believe that it is possible for monsters to be in the wardrobe.

- Hug and kiss your children. Most child molesters never had good hugs and kisses: in one American study eighty per cent were found to have been molested themselves as children, either physically or sexually. For children, those appropriate touches, hugs and kisses are the best gifts we can give them.

In spite of taking precautions, it is not always possible to prevent a child being harmed. Remember that if someone harms a child, it is always the offender's fault, and never the fault of the child or the person trying to keep the child safe.

HELPING TEENAGERS TO PROTECT THEMSELVES

While parents want their teenagers to be independent, it is obvious that this group also needs preventive tactics to deal with common assault problems. The most frequent problem at this age is the acquaintance or date rape. Too often teenagers are afraid to hurt someone's feelings, or do not want to look foolish in front of their friends, or just do not expect someone they know to betray their trust. Therefore they may end up in a dangerous situation not knowing what to do.

Susan, eighteen years old, was at a staff Christmas party with people from the firm where she had worked for over a year. After she had drunk too much, her twenty-seven-year-old manager insisted upon driving her home. He easily persuaded her to stop and have a cup of coffee at his flat so that her parents would not see her in such a state. Once in the flat, he threatened her, raped her seven times and left her unconscious. She woke up after he had passed out, left the flat, took a taxi home and never went back to her job. She also never told anyone or reported it to the police because, 'I went with him to the flat. The police would not believe me if I said it was rape'. Although she knows her parents would believe her, she is afraid that her father would kill the man and that her parents would worry about her every time she went out. Susan is still angry, hurt, confused and frightened by the incident.

What you should discuss

Setting limits

By deciding what needs and limits they have, teenagers will be in a better position to determine if they are getting into a situation beyond their control. These limits will change depending upon the person they are with and upon the teenager's age and maturity. By thinking about their own boundaries, teenagers will begin to test and trust their judgement, an important tool in keeping safe.

Setting limits can include deciding what to do if asked by friends or acquaintances to go along with something teenagers like or do not really like or feel comfortable about. What if a group of friends want to go to the cinema, have a party, go to a pub, get drunk, shoplift, try drugs, go to a disco, go somewhere for a 'kiss and cuddle', or find some girls or boys 'ready for action'? Teenagers should think about what they want before the opportunities are presented to them.

Communicating these limits

Teenagers need to be told to communicate their limits to others: boyfriends, girlfriends, friends or acquaintances. Although peer group pressure is great at this age, planning in advance makes saying no easier. For younger teenagers, using parents as an excuse sometimes helps: 'My Mum won't let me...' Parents should not be misled by their teenager's rebellious poses; many teenagers are secretly grateful to place the 'blame' on their parents.

Trusting intuition

Often teenagers do not trust their own feelings and judgement. Though they may sense they are getting into a difficult situation, they have not thought out what to do or do not want to appear silly in front of friends, so they go

along until it is too late. By learning to trust that inner feeling, teenagers can avoid many potential problems.

Mike was talked into having a party while his parents were away for the evening. His friends said that they would help clear up and that his parents would 'never know'. Though he felt uncomfortable, Mike agreed because he wanted to be part of the group. Everything went well until a neighbourhood group of troublemakers gatecrashed. Mike knew immediately he should get help, but thought that by handling the situation himself he could avoid getting into difficulty with his parents.

The troublemakers began to beat the boys, molest some of the girls and wreck the house. Only then did one of the boys telephone the police, ignoring the protesting host who said that his parents would 'kill him' for allowing the party to take place. Had Mike trusted his judgement and refused to have the party, none of this would have happened.

Trusting feelings includes taking action in case a young person, or indeed anyone, feels they are being followed. If this seems to be happening, they should immediately walk towards a place with people, like a shop or play area in a park. If there are houses nearby, they should go up to the door of one and either pretend to ring the bell or ring the bell if the person continues to follow. They should have no hesitation in picking up a rock and breaking a window if this is necessary to get help. A broken window can always be fixed and it does bring attention! Young people need to know that parents will support them should this kind of situation arise.

Being aware of the behaviour of others

If someone is acting in an inappropriate way, it is best to keep a safe distance. For example, if a person in the group is making inappropriate jokes or comments, drinking too much, or not listening and offending others, then tell teenagers not to get involved. If another person acts in an over familiar way, gets too close in a way which makes them uncomfortable, or begins touching them, teenagers should be told to say no forcefully and get help.

Avoiding unnecessary risks: hitch hiking

Given the fact that people can be raped, sexually assaulted, robbed, or murdered when hitch hiking, the only sensible advice is Don't Do It.

Saying no and meaning it

One of the most commonly held myths is that when a girl says no, she means yes (see true/false questionnaire on pages 161–70). To avoid any misunderstanding, girls should be told to look the person in the eye and say no in a loud, firm voice. They should make sure their body language conveys the same message. Teenage girls should remember that they have the right to say no and that kissing and cuddling should not be regarded as an open invitation to have sexual intercourse.

Becoming angry

Many people become frozen with fear and cannot think in a dangerous situation. Anger helps to focus energy and convert thoughts into action. Tell teenagers to think 'I don't deserve this' and use whatever force is necessary to get out of the difficulty. Teenagers should realise that by acting quickly and decisively, they may be saving themselves from potential harm.

> Jenny had been jogging in the park, wearing her Walkman, and failed to hear the older teenage boy who approached from behind and dragged her to a secluded area. She saw people walking by, but they could not see her. She was terrified and could not remember anything from the self-defence class she was taking. However, when the boy tried to pull down her shorts,

she became angry 'I haven't done anything to him,' she thought. 'He has no right to do this to me!' With that, she yelled a deep, loud scream, pushed him hard and ran away towards the path. He was startled and ran in another direction. Jenny later remarked that her anger gave her strength she didn't know she had.

The Walkman is, incidentally, one hazard that parents did not have to contend with as teenagers – there are some advantages in growing older! But teens should be made aware that it is not just their possible future lack of hearing that is of concern. Wearing a Walkman might signify to an attacker that the person is not aware of what is happening. As in Jenny's case, it could have harmful consequences.

Learning self-defence

Taking a self-defence course is a good idea for those who are willing to do the necessary work and practise what they have been taught. For most teenagers or adults, knowing and practising three or four techniques would be more helpful than having so much information that it is all forgotten in a crisis. Learning how to get out of a hold, where the pressure points are on the body and how to kick, bite or hit to get away would be useful information for most people: Check what courses there are in your local area (see page 133).

Telling a trusted adult

If a teenager is raped or molested, he or she often does not tell, fearing censure by friends, humiliation or disbelief. Teenagers, too, need a network of trusted adults to whom they can turn. Parents can help teenagers work out a list or teenagers can do it on their own. They should be told to keep telling until they receive help. Adults also must learn to give help without censure. One enlightened father has told all of his children that if they ever get into a situation they cannot handle, they can telephone him and he will pick them up, no questions asked.

Knowing that the offender is responsible

This is an important message because most teenagers will not tell parents if they are attacked for fear that they will be blamed. They may also blame themselves as many victims of assault do: 'I did not follow the rules, so this is my fault'. Parents and others who deal with teenagers should emphasise that it is the offender's fault.

The facts about sexual abuse

Since many people are misinformed about the realities of sexual abuse, dicussing facts will lead to a better understanding of the problems. If boys and girls examine the issues together so that the message is the same for both, then they can begin to understand what to expect from each other and communicate in an open and honest way.

The questionnaires on pages 139–70 can be used to introduce the subject. Although the majority of the answers are straightforward, the questionnaires should be used to stimulate discussion and not as an exam with 'right' and 'wrong' answers. In the questionnaire for younger teenagers, for example, the answer to question 11 about never fighting back could be true or false depending upon the circumstances.

Teenagers should be given the opportunity to discuss the answers with friends, parents or school personnel such as teachers, school nurses or health visitors. (See also Tips for teenagers when looking for part-time jobs, pages 113–15.)

HOW TEACHERS AND OTHER ADULTS CAN HELP

With the increasing concern about children's safety, teachers and other adults who work with children are asking how they can help. Teaching personal safety covers a wide range of concerns: from getting lost to being bullied, or being approached by strangers or by someone known to the child who is intent on harm. The lessons can be fun and children often enjoy them.

Before talking to children about personal safety, it is essential to enlist the support of parents and other people in the community, for several reasons. Community sensitivities must be taken into account, and classroom discussions must be kept within the guidelines that are acceptable to parents and the school. There are many components in teaching children how to keep safe, and it is not always necessary to include every one. For example, there may be some religious or cultural objections to children trying to defend themselves in a physical way against an attacker. Another important factor is that talking about good touches and bad touches could lead to a child disclosing that abuse has already occurred. If that happens, the teacher will need to draw on the back-up network of community services for support.

Many of the ideas at the beginning of this book can be used in schools, nurseries, play associations and youth groups. The following ideas for specific age groups are included here as suggestions for some additional ways to work with children. (For more detailed information about introducing a comprehensive programme into schools, contact Kidscape.)

Pre-school children

One way which has worked quite well with young children is to introduce the topic of safety by explaining that keeping safe means taking care. Ask them to think up ways of taking care of themselves. Their ideas may include:

- Washing hair
- Brushing teeth
- Taking baths
- Eating
- Drinking
- Going to the toilet

Talking about pets is another good way to bring up the concept of taking care of someone or something. Ask your children to tell you about a toy or something special like a favourite blanket that belongs to them. Use this as a way to explain that their bodies are also special and belong to them.

Discuss touching and some of the other ideas mentioned earlier in this book. Tickling is a good way to bring up the subject of touching as most young children can understand 'liking or not liking' tickling.

Have children make a hug list. This can be done verbally with very young children by asking them from whom they like hugs and kisses. Grannies come top of most lists, with Mummy, Daddy and Grandpa closely following. Four-year-old James declared that he liked his dog's 'lick hugs'. Children can be encouraged to draw pictures or paste up photos on some paper for their hug list.

These conversations with children, brought up occasionally, begin to help them with the concept of trusting their own feelings about what they do and don't like.

Use stories like *The Tale of Peter Rabbit* to introduce the idea that children should tell, even if they have broken a family rule. Peter broke the family rule about invading Mr. McGregor's garden and was almost made into rabbit pie, like his father. He did not tell his mother how he had lost his coat because he should not have been in the garden in the first place. In addition, the concept of self-reliance can be introduced by explaining how Peter used his wits to escape from the garden.

Use puppets or dolls to portray what happens in a playground, such as one child taking away a toy from another. Ask the children what they would do, how they would help each other and how they would get adult assistance.

Primary school children

Here is one method by which children can be taught to protect themselves. Most children have had the experience of being confronted by a bully. The teacher or worker can introduce the subject of bullying by using an example such as:

John is playing in the park when an older, bigger boy approaches and demands John's pocket money. John gives the bully his money and is therefore unsuccessful in defending himself.

Then discuss how John felt, how the bully felt and explain that John had his right to be safe taken away. Ask the children what they would do in this situation. Be prepared for the children wanting to punch the bully on the nose and asking if that would solve the problem. 'Wouldn't the bully then hit back?' Ask the children about telling an adult and if that would mean they were telling tales, as discussed in the first part of this book. If none of the children mentions taking a friend along, suggest that having a friend, brother or sister helping to say no makes people feel stronger.

If the question of the bully having a weapon is raised, explain it is far better to give the bully the money, but that they should definitely tell an adult what happened.

By relating the problem of bullies to illustrate the concept of personal safety, the teacher or worker has made the idea of the right to be safe clear to the children.

Young teenagers

Having begun the discussion by talking about rights, give the questionnaire on pages 151–6 to the children (see page 149 for information on how to use the questionnaire). Do not collect the papers; discuss the answers which will take at least half an hour. Continue by either telling or eliciting stories of bullies and strangers, and encourage the children to talk about how they would cope in various situations. What to do if approached by a known adult can be introduced when the children are ready. One way this can be done is by using a story about a girl (or boy) who has been babysitting for an aunt and uncle. When the uncle takes the babysitter home, he tries to kiss her and she rebuffs him. The uncle then tells her that the incident must be kept a secret. Discussion should focus on the issues of secrecy and who to tell.

Older teenagers

Use the questionnaire on pages 161–70 and discuss the answers. (See page 159 for guidance on how to use the questionnaire). Do not collect the papers. Relate the story on page 37 about Susan and ask the children who was at fault. This can lead to further discussion about responsibility and guilt, trusting feelings, setting limits and the other topics mentioned in chapter 1, 'Helping teenagers to protect themselves'. The teacher may wish to give lessons in basic self-defence.

Reporting cases of suspected sexual abuse

Anyone who works with children should also be aware of the danger signs and who to contact for help. Although local guidelines vary for reporting suspected cases of child sexual abuse, concerned adults are advised to contact their local social services for suggestions on the appropriate action to take. The help organisations listed in this book on pages 124–7 are also available to give advice. The dangers signs listed on pages 51–7 provide teachers or workers with identifiable physical and emotional characteristics they should pay attention to when they suspect child abuse.

Some children will already have been sexually abused, but have not yet told. It is important, therefore, in discussing these issues with children to make sure they are not made to feel guilty. In one workshop, an eleven-year-old girl started crying and later disclosed that she had been sexually assaulted by an older cousin two years previously. She felt guilty for having kept the secret and for not having said no.

When talking with children, say that sometimes children may be placed in a situation in which they cannot say no or get help. Emphasise that this is not their fault, and that children who have survived abuse and not told are very brave, but nevertheless they should try to get help from an adult. If a child reveals having been sexually abused, use the suggestions listed on pages 61–71 to help deal with the disclosure. Promise to do everything in your power to protect the child, but do not promise that what is said will be kept secret. You will need the help of other people when dealing with cases of sexual abuse. This should never be the responsibility of one person, which is why the support of other professionals is so important.

The use of videos

There are now many videos for children about keeping safe from sexual abuse. Well-meaning adults may be tempted to use a video to introduce children to the issues.

This method may seem to allow an admittedly difficult subject to be dealt with in a non-threatening way. If video can work as an aid for teaching maths and science, why not for teaching prevention of sexual abuse?

Teachers who use videos as teaching aids have usually been prepared in the discipline being discussed and use the video to reinforce and/or follow up a lesson, not to introduce the concepts. Since most teachers have no preparation in preventing child sexual abuse, videos should not be used to introduce the ideas to children.

Videos also keep the subject at arm's length. Adults may think that children understand what to do because they have seen a video. But it is extremely difficult to introduce the ideas about safe and unsafe touching in the passive medium of video. Children will have a lot of questions to ask and the discussion needs to be continuous and interactive to ensure that children understand the messages. There is no substitute for talking with children, particularly in an area as sensitive as this.

Nevertheless, some videos can be useful as part of a follow-up lesson after children have taken part in an interactive learning process. A video could then be used as a tool, but not the primary means, for continuing discussion and reinforcing the message of personal safety.

MORE SUGGESTIONS FOR TEACHERS AND WORKERS

- Arrange a parent's meeting. Parental involvement and support is essential.
- Discuss how to get help when a child needs adult assistance.
- Teach children that you give them permission to say no to keep safe.
- Talk about the difference between safe 'good' secrets and unsafe 'bad' secrets.
- Help children to establish a network of trusted adults.
- Discuss with children the difference between bribes and gifts.
- Help children to learn how to deal with bullies.
- Help children to learn how to deal with approaches not only by strangers but also by people they know who may harm them.
- Keep an incident log in order to ensure that incidents of children being approached by strangers are reported and centrally monitored.
- Be aware of and follow local procedures.

2 DEALING WITH CHILD SEXUAL ABUSE

HOW TO RECOGNISE THE DANGER SIGNS

In most cases of sexual abuse there are no obvious physical signs and symptoms. This often makes it difficult to find out if a child has been abused, especially if the child has not told of the abuse.

There are, however, some common characteristics shared by children who have been abused which can indicate that something is wrong. Being alert to these signs and symptoms can help, especially if the child is also displaying a hopeless, watchful or fearful attitude. People who deal with children who have been abused call this attitude one of 'frozen watchfulness', as if the child is not engaging in life and is wary about what will happen next.

Since it is difficult for children to talk about what has happened to them, the clues that they give through their behaviour may be the only way we have of finding out what is troubling them. While many of these behavioural patterns are normal for growing children, it is important to remember that they can also be indicative of sexual abuse and should therefore be investigated. In Appendix 5 are listed some possible signs of physical and emotional abuse, as well as neglect. Unfortunately in many cases there may be more than one kind of abusing occuring.

Children under the age of five may:

- Become insecure or cling to parents in a fearful way
- Show extreme fear of a particular person
- Cry hysterically when their nappy is changed
- Become hysterical when clothing is removed, particularly underclothes
- Have some physical signs in the genitals area: smell of semen, etc.
- Have soreness or bleeding in the throat, anal or genital areas
- Regress to a much younger behavioural pattern
- Behave in a way sexually inappropriate to their age, being obsessed with sexual matters as opposed to normal exploration (see pages 53–7)
- Stare blankly, seem unhappy, confused, sad
- Become withdrawn, stop eating, have chronic nightmares, begin wetting again when previously dry
- Play out sexual acts in too knowledgable a way with dolls or other children
- Produce drawings of sex organs such as erect penises
- Stop enjoying activities with other children, such as stories or games
- Seem to be bothered or worried, but won't tell why as if keeping a secret
- Change from being happy and active to being withdrawn and fearful
- Repeat obscene words or phrases said by the abuser
- Say repeatedly that they are bad, dirty or wicked
- Become aggressive and hurtful

One mother noticed that her four-year-old child suddenly started exhibiting several of these conditions. She checked into all the possibilities she could think of, but to no avail. Her son was particularly troubled whenever he went to play at their neighbour's flat. He would come home in a bad mood, refuse to eat and go to his room. He muttered to himself that he was dirty and rude.

After some questioning, the mother found out that the lodger had been making her son and her neighbour's child 'play dirty games' which the children were told to keep secret. These children were also told that their mothers would hate them and would send them away if they told, so they were frightened to tell. It was only by observing the changes in her son that the abuse was stopped.

Children from the age of five to twelve may:

- Hint about secrets they cannot tell

- Say that a friend has a problem

- Ask you if you will keep a secret if they tell you something

- Begin lying, stealing, blatantly cheating in the hope of being caught

- Have unexplained sources of money

- Have terrifying dreams

- Start wetting themselves

- Exhibit sudden inexplicable changes in behaviour, such as becoming aggressive or withdrawn

- Stop enjoying previously liked activities, such as music, sports, art, scouts or guides, going to summer camp, gym club

- Be reluctant to undress for gym

- Become fearful of or refuse to see certain adults for no

apparent reason; dislike of a particular babysitter, relative or other adult

- Act in a sexual way inappropriate to their age
- Draw sexually explicit pictures depicting some act of abuse
- Seem to be keeping secret something which is worrying them
- Have urinary infections, bleeding or soreness in the genital or anal areas
- Have soreness or bleeding in the throat
- Have chronic ailments, such as stomach or headaches
- Take over the parent role at home, seem old beyond their years (if victim of incest)
- Develop eating disorders, such as anorexia or buliminia
- Become severely depressed, even attempt suicide
- Have a poor self-image, self-mutilate
- Continually run away
- Regress to younger behaviour, such thumb-sucking, surrounding themselves with previously discarded cuddly toys
- Show discomfort walking
- Say that they are no good, dirty, rotten
- Be wary, watchful
- Repeat obscene words or phrases which may have been said during the abuse
- Attempt to sexually abuse another child
- Talk or write about sexual matters
- Find hundreds of excuses not to go home or to a friend's

house after school (places where abuse may be happening)

An eight-year-old girl suddenly became withdrawn and unhappy, refusing to play with any of her friends. She said she was ugly and started pulling out bits of her hair and biting herself. The child's teacher became increasingly concerned and tried talking with her. But the girl refused to talk. The teacher had a conference with her mother and discovered that the child was acting the same way at home.

After much discussion, it was discovered that her grandfather had sexually abused the child on a recent visit. It was one incident and it was the only time it had happened to her, though it was subsequently found out that he had abused three other grandchildren for a number of years. The children had never told anyone as the grandfather had told them that he would go to prison if they did. The child was very badly affected by the abuse and needed counselling over a long period of time.

Young people from the age of thirteen onwards may:

- Be chronically depressed
- Be suicidal
- Use drugs or drink to excess
- Self-mutilate, show self-hatred
- Have unexplained pregnancies
- Experience memory loss
- Become anorexic or buliminic
- Run away frequently
- Be inappropriately seductive
- Be fearful about certain people like relatives or friends
- Assume the role of parents in the house to such an

extent that they do all the cooking, cleaning, child-minding and are taking care of everyone's needs except their own

- Not be allowed to go out on dates or have friends round
- Have soreness, bleeding in the genital or anal areas or in the throat
- Find excuses not to go home or to a particular place
- Have recurring nightmares, be afraid of the dark
- Be unable to concentrate, seem to be in a world of their own
- Have a 'friend who has a problem' and then tell about the abuse of the friend
- Have chronic ailments such as stomach and headaches
- Sexually abuse a child, sibling or friend
- Exhibit a sudden change in school/work habits, become truant
- Be withdrawn, isolated, or excessively worried
- Have outbursts of anger or irritability
- Be fearful of undressing for gym
- Have unexplained sums of money

Fifteen-year-old Karen had been sexually abused for years by her stepfather. He told her she was his 'special girl', bought her presents and gave her large sums of money. She had the major responsibilities in the house and was never allowed to go out with friends, girls or boys. She was told that if she disclosed the abuse to anyone, the family would fall apart and she would be the cause.

Because the abuse had been long term, she did not show sudden changes in behaviour, but had exhibited several signs through the years. She had attempted suicide on two occasions, had become anorexic, could not concentrate in school, was often depressed and continually had health problems.

Karen's plight should have been uncovered years previously, given the number of alarming signals. The abuse was only stopped because an alert gym teacher recognised that Karen's symptoms could be indicative of sexual abuse. Unfortunately, Karen's stepfather did not admit to the abuse and her mother turned against her. Although Karen disclosed the abuse, she later retracted. Karen went to live with her grandmother, but she still needs long-term therapy to come to terms with what has happened. Perhaps the outcome would have been better had the abuse been recognised earlier, but we will never know.

It should also be noted that some children and young people who are abused go to great lengths to conceal what is happening and somehow manage not to show any behaviour associated with the abuse.

WHAT TO DO IF YOU SUSPECT ABUSE

If you are worried that a child has been sexually abused and has not told anyone, first make sure that you are prepared should the child confirm your fears. Often parents and other adults hope that there will be another explanation for the symptoms or behaviour which is causing concern. Before talking with a child, read this book and particularly chapters 1 and 2.

With younger children, one approach is to first talk with the child about hugs, kisses, good touches, secrets and telling as discussed earlier in this book. Do this gradually (over a period of days, if necessary), and without communicating your anxieties to the child. When you feel the child is ready, ask directly if someone has touched him or her in a way which the child either did not like or which hurt or was uncomfortable. The direct approach, made calmly, is important because children seldom respond to indirect questioning as they do not understand what is being asked.

If there is a specific physical indication of an assault, point to that part of the body and ask if anyone has touched the child there. Remain calm and do not press the child for information. Let the child tell at his or her own pace.

> One mother related that her three-year-old daughter often had vaginal redness after visiting an older cousin's house. The mother did not want to question her daughter because she did not know how to begin and did not want to frighten the child.
>
> After preparing both herself and her daughter to discuss the problem in a calm way, the mother found out that the cousin was sexually assaulting her child. As do most offenders, the cousin denied it when confronted by the child's parents.

Each adult must decide according to the circumstances how to proceed in the best interests of the child. In this case the child was supported and helped at home, and the parents decided not to bring in medical or professional help. They immediately broke off all contact with the cousin, but since their major concern was not to get the child involved in a possible court appearance, they did not contact the police. Another parent might try to have the offender put in prison to protect other children, and contact the police.

> An eight-year-old boy became increasingly unhappy about visiting his maths tutor. Because the child did not like maths, his parents thought he was reluctant to study. This was confirmed by the tutor. After several months of increasing tension, during which time the child began to wet his bed and became aggressive and sullen, the father decided to talk to him about his behaviour.
>
> The child finally explained that the tutor had been making him play 'secret games' and remove his clothes. When asked why he had not told anyone, the boy said the tutor told him that no one would believe

him and, if questioned, the tutor would say he was lying. The boy was trapped in what seemed to be an impossible situation.

In this case the police were called, the child was believed by his parents and the police, but because of the lack of medical evidence and the tutor's denial, he was not prosecuted. But the abuse did stop and the child was given support. The concern in these cases is that the offender will go on to assault new victims.

Another parent became worried when her daughter, aged nine, began to have bad dreams, surrounded herself with some previously discarded cuddly toys before going to sleep at night and seemed to be suddenly reluctant to be in the sitting room in the evenings. The girl was not having any difficulties at school and showed no changes in behaviour outside the home.

After eliminating all other possible causes she could think of, the mother asked her daughter if anyone had been touching her in a way which made her feel unsafe or if anyone had asked her to keep secrets from her mum. The child said no and the mother was greatly relieved. But the behaviour causing concern continued, so the mother continued to ask about it. This went on for a month, until the mother finally said, 'Are you frightened to tell me your secret because you think I might be angry or not love you, because no matter what the problem is, I promise that I will try to help and that I won't be angry with you or blame you.'

The child finally revealed that the lodger had been interfering with her, but that she thought it was her fault because it did not hurt and even felt good sometimes. She alternately hated him and liked him and did not know what to do.

These feelings make it even more difficult for a child to tell and get help.

In this case the man was arrested, found to have a history of abusing children, and was imprisoned.

Although it is particularly difficult if the abuse is happening within the family, the concerned adult must seek help for the child. When the suspected offender is the child's parent, step-parent, or other close family member, the mother or another adult can use the same method for preparing to talk with the child. Because of the effects that this will have on the child and the family, it may be useful to get professional advice in advance. Several of the help organisations listed on pages 124–7 of this book will listen and make suggestions, on an anonymous basis if requested.

If the child does say that abuse has taken place, the subsequent safety and well-being of the child must be the first consideration. No child should be left alone with a suspected offender.

Talking with teenagers is often more difficult, as they have usually experienced adult disbelief and are reluctant to tell for fear of not being believed. They are also much more aware of the consequences of telling, especially if the abuser is either well known to them or within the family. If they were assaulted by a friend or acquaintance, it may have happened when they were breaking a rule. They are often afraid that they will be punished for the assault and that they will never be allowed to go out again.

Although asking directly can sometimes lead to a disclosure of sexual abuse, most teenagers will choose who they will tell and when. Therefore keeping the lines of communication open and showing that you are ready to listen and not to blame can be very effective ways to help teenagers or children to talk.

Many people are unsure of how to deal with suspected cases of sexual abuse, or what to do in the event of a disclosure. Dealing with these cases is never easy. However, you must take steps to find out whether abuse is taking place in order to protect the child and to keep other children safe.

The long-term effects of abuse on a child's life depend upon the severity and duration of the attack and how the child is then cared for by family, friends and/or professionals. Some children, especially those blamed and rejected by their families, carry the scars for life and never form loving relationships as adults. Yet children are resilient and with proper care and support the healing will begin. Children who are supported have a much better chance of coping and eventually establishing stable relationships.

WHAT TO DO IF AN ASSAULT OCCURS

Children cannot be supervised twenty-four hours a day. Even by taking all precautions and giving children strategies for staying safe, you cannot guarantee that they will not be harmed. If your child is assaulted it often results in feelings of outrage and helplessness: 'If only I had picked her up from school this wouldn't have happened' or 'If only I had realised why he was acting that way, I could have stopped it from going on'. The ensuing guilt or even the reactions of other people can perpetuate the feeling that somehow you could have prevented the assault.

Since most children do not want to cause pain to someone they love, they may try to protect you. The reaction of the adult will often determine how much the child will tell. A child may just reveal a little of the problem at a time to see what you do. The following suggestions may prove helpful:

- Stay calm. Try not to transmit your anger, shock and embarrassment to your child. Remaining calm will help lessen the effect of the trauma. It will help your child to know you are now in control of a situation he or she could not cope with alone. If you have had a similar experience in childhood, this may be very difficult to do. When seeking professional help for yourself and your child (see below), you may want to talk privately about what happened to you in the past.

- Believe your child. Children rarely lie about sexual abuse unless they are denying it has happened to protect someone.

- Reassure your child. Children often feel responsible for or guilty about the incident; emphasise that it is not the child's fault. Tell your child you are glad he or she told you.

- Encourage the child to talk. Question gently and make sure that your child knows that you are supportive. Do not push your child to give you information, but show that you are prepared to listen.

- Report the incident to the authorities. Sometimes this is not an easy decision. The age of the child, the seriousness of the offence and the possible effects of a court case are mentioned by parents as causes for concern when deciding whether to report. The adult must also consider the danger to other children if the offender is allowed to go free. When the abuse is reported, explain to the child that a policeman or woman, or another professional person would like to talk with him or her, and that the person's job is to help protect children. Stay with the child during the interview.

- Praise your child for having survived the attack. Explain that he or she had no choice at the time of the offence. Say that you are glad your child survived and that he or she is now safe. This often helps a child to come to terms with the question, 'What did I do wrong?' Later you can talk about how to keep safe in the future and teach preventive skills.

- Seek medical attention, if necessary. Explain to your child what the doctor will do and why. Make sure that the doctor is compassionate. Privately ask the doctor to reassure your child that his or her body is all right, despite the incident. Stay with your child during the examination, if possible and appropriate.

- Seek help. Professional counselling or self-help groups may help to lessen the traumatic effect of the incident.

- Try not to change the routine of home or school. During times of stress this is helpful because it provides a structure to work within and should faciltate the healing process. If the offender is a family member, it must be decided what is in the best interests of the child.

- Reiterate that it is the offender's fault. Never tell your child that what happened was naughty or dirty. If you do, the child will assume that he or she is somehow to blame. Try not to make judgemental statements about the offender, because in some cases the child may have mixed feelings about the person. This is particularly true if the offender is either a member of the child's family or well known to the child. If necessary, say that the person was wrong to have done this or that the person has a problem and needs help. For younger children it might help to explain that the person was naughty or compare the offence to a burglar taking something that he or she had no right to take.

- Use puppets or dolls. With young children you may want to use toys to help them to discuss their feelings. This can also be helpful in teaching them some of the preventive techniques mentioned earlier.

Violent assaults

It is always difficult to deal with the abuse of a child, but when a child is badly beaten, as well as sexually assaulted or raped, the trauma for the child and family can be overwhelming.

'When they allowed me in to see my daughter, I fainted. There was my eleven-year-old with her face so badly beaten that I couldn't even recognise her. She had broken bones and terrible internal injuries and I was helpless to do anything. I wanted to kill the person who had done this. I knew we had almost lost her and I kept going over and over how this could have happened and why. I was furious with myself and my husband for not protecting her, hated the man who had done this, and angry that this had happened to my child. Our world was shattered.'

In coping with cases like this, some of the suggestions listed above will be helpful. In addition, the police and medical authorities will certainly be involved and a full-scale investigation will be put into motion. In some ways these actions and the immediate intervention can be helpful, for they provide a structure and give the feeling that 'something is being done'. However, most families are left to cope with the after-effects of an assault, often without help.

If the family and child are not offered professional counselling, the parents should approach either the social services or their GP for the names of counsellors, psychiatrists or psychologists. Friends can help by listening and not turning away. When a child is violently assaulted, people sometimes find it difficult to know what to say, so they say nothing or pretend nothing has happened.

But many survivors of child sexual abuse say that often well-meaning silence of people around them only made them feel guilty or ashamed. They were not helped to express their feelings, which led to them taking responsibility for what happened. One person who had been raped as a child said:

'Whenever I tried to talk to my Mum, she just cried and said she was sorry. It frightened me when she cried, so I stopped talking about it. I wanted her to hug me and tell me that she loved me and that I wouldn't always feel so sad. I guess I wanted to be reassured that my whole life wasn't ruined.'

Talking and listening will help the child to come to terms with what has happened. Sexual assault is rarely forgotten, but it does not have to ruin a person's life. Give the child time to talk about his or her feelings by saying that you would like to listen and help. Allow the child to talk at his or her own pace, however long it takes. If your child feels angry or fearful, help him or her to express these emotions. This may also help your child to ask questions about what happened.

If the child asks, 'Why did that person do this?', one answer might be that the person had a problem and that it was not the child's fault. Say that you are glad that he or she is alive and that you will try to help them get better as fast as possible. Admit that you do not have all the answers. There often are no answers as to why it happened, but continually reassuring the child that you love him or her and that they were not responsible will help the healing process.

This process can often be lengthy, both for the child and the family. Other children in the family may need extra reassurance, as well, for they can feel angry, hurt, fearful or even jealous because of the attention being paid to their sibling.

What next?

If your child is sexually abused and/or violently assaulted, you will need help and support, particularly if the adults in the family blame each other or if they react in different ways. For example, in one family where a child had survived a violent sexual assault, the mother needed time to weep and talk, while the father reacted by becoming very busy. They both resented the way the other dealt with their emotions and were unable to support each other or their child. Deal with your feelings in a way that is comfortable for you, but try not to impose them on others. If you are a single parent, enlist the help of friends or family.

It will take time for the child and other family members

to come to terms with what has happened, for there are no magic ways to get through the trauma of a child being sexually abused.

The after-effects of abuse

The way that children respond after having been abused varies greatly according to:

- How the abuse is perceived by the child – as painful, worrying, scary, feeling good, horrible, etc.
- The age of the child
- The relationship of the child to the abuser
- The kind of abuse
- The severity and duration of the abuse
- The reactions of those around the child
- The kind of help the child and family receives after the abuse

Children's reactions range from being withdrawn, angry or sullen to confusion, aggression, guilt, anxiety, or to self-control and seeming indifference.

How to deal with the after-effects

To deal with the after-effects of abuse, most children will need some therapy or counselling. If you are unable to get therapy, expert guidance or any other kind of help for children who have been abused, there are some things that parents and other caring adults might do to help:

- Explain that you will always be willing to listen should the child ever want to talk
- Be reassuring when talking with the child, and stress that it wasn't the child's fault. The earlier guidelines on pages 61–3 are still relevant
- Have plasticine around and use it in play as a possible

way for the child to express feelings

- Use drawing too. Try to encourage the child to draw a happy face or a sad face and talk about why the face feels that way. This can allow the child to keep a safe distance, but also bring out concerns

- Encourage fingerpainting, playing with water and sand, punching bags, pounding nails into wood, physical activity that allows pent up anxiety to escape

- Fun excursions can also be therapeutic

Abused children have often been left powerless and without good feelings about themselves. To help children gain confidence and become more self-assertive:

- Use the 'NO' exercise on pages 20–2

- Praise the child for doing something well, perhaps clearing up or setting the table

- Involve him or her in making decisions, even such minor things as which jumper they want to wear

- Encourage the child to experiment and be creative

- Put up their work on the refrigerator or a wall and comment about how you like it

- Allow them time and space to themselves – don't smother them

If your child expresses bad feelings, don't minimise what is said. For example, a child may say that he or she is dirty or ugly and you might reply that it isn't true. The problem is that it might be true for the child and reflect how the child is feeling. Instead of denying those feelings, acknowledge them by saying: 'It must be difficult for you to feel that way. Let's talk about it.' This gives the child an opening to get out some of those bad feelings. Certainly tell the child that you don't feel that way.

Since many victims of abuse have not got a sense of their own bodies, do body awareness exercises like:

- Moving to music
- Drawing self-portraits
- Drawing a full-size outline of the child on lining wallpaper and encouraging the child to colour it in
- Looking at their own baby pictures
- Looking in the mirror and telling what they see

It is important to help your child establish control over any inappropriate behaviour, such as compulsive masturbation in public. Help by being firm about what is acceptable and consult teachers and anyone else who might help to set limits. Explain to your child that, although the abuser said the behaviour was all right, the abuser was wrong.

Children may regress to younger behaviour patterns, such as cuddling an old teddy bear or sucking their thumbs. This may be comforting and should be allowed as it may help them come to terms with what has happened.

- Continue to be cuddly with the child, but *only* if the child feels comfortable. Sometimes a child who has been abused withdraws from physical contact. In this case don't force it, but make it clear that you would like a hug or kiss when the child is ready. This might not be easy for the adult who wants to comfort.

- If you are the father or a close male friend of a child who has been sexually abused, the above applies especially. When a child has been abused by a man, the father sometimes becomes reluctant to hug or kiss the child for fear of it 'being harmful' to the child. If you have had a loving relationship and you withdraw, it could prove even more difficult for the child to make a recovery.

- Tell the child that you love and/or like him or her. Children often feel that they are not worth loving after being sexually abused.

- If the victim of the abuse is a boy, he may be worried about how the abuse affects his masculinity. He may think that he is now gay or that he was abused because he looked weak. He will need assurance that it wasn't his fault and that being abused by a man does not 'turn you into a homosexual'. It may help to say that even very strong adult men have experienced this sometimes. The same applies to cases in which a girl is abused by a woman.

- If a boy has been abused by a woman, he will need the same kind of help and assurance that any victim of sexual abuse needs. There has been a tendency to dismiss these cases by saying the boy was 'lucky to be initiated', although the effects can be quite devastating.

- The same applies to gay teenagers who have been sexually abused. They will also be experiencing considerable trauma and be in need of support. There are organisations which can help (see list of help groups pages 124–7) if you feel unable to talk about it.

- Make time for yourself and find support. If you feel enraged, angry, vengeful, guilty, embarrassed or fearful, you need an outlet. Sexual abuse affects not only the child, but the whole family. It is the most difficult when the abuser is known or a family member and changes take place in family life. Although the child's interests are the most important consideration, the opportunity to assist the child is greater if the person helping is coping as well as possible.

- If you are still seething about what has happened, try if possible to do something constructive. Join one of the groups that helps others, try to activate a prevention programme in your child's school, write letters to parliament about the treatment of child victims, join pressure groups to change laws, start a self-help group or anything that you can think will help children and yourself.

- Help your child decide about what to say to friends. Sometimes children who are abused tell too many friends who do not know how to handle this information. Some children are then hurt when their friends misuse the child's confidence.

- If you are the teacher of a child who has been abused, many of the above suggestions may be helpful when the child returns to class. It is probably helpful to find a quiet moment to say you're glad to have the child back with you and that you are willing to listen if the child wants to talk about anything that is troubling him or her. Then try to ensure that the child is reintegrated into the class. If you can, arrange a 'time out' place where the child can go if feeling tearful at first. The school nurse can be a good ally.

- If the assault has been fairly well known, then it may be necessary to chat with the children before the child comes back to class. This obviously depends upon the age of the children. With young children, it is sometimes enough to say that 'Johnny has been hurt or ill and is coming back today'. With older children a caution to be helpful without being nosey might be in order. With teens, a word about realising it could happen to anyone and consider how you would like to be treated now could make the transition easier. Guidance should be taken from both the child and the family or therapist where possible.

- If the abuse is not public knowledge, then nothing should be said unless it is at the request and in the best interests of the child.

- If the child is concerned about AIDS, in addition to the concern about sexual abuse, see chapter 4 for some suggestions and look under 'Where to Get Help' (pp. 127-8) for organisations which may be able to answer your questions.

When helping children overcome the problems related to

being sexually abused, it is also important not to try to be a therapist. This could cause more harm than good, however well meaning. It is best to be available, listen and help the child express his or her feelings, but to maintain your relationship as a parent, teacher or other caring adult.

Finally, keep trying to get expert help by asking your doctor or paedatrician, the social services or other helping agencies for advice and referrals. Even if there is a waiting list, put your name on it and keep checking until your child and you feel satisfied that everything possible has been done.

Part 2: Drugs, Alcohol, AIDS, Bullies and Other Dangers: Strategies for Keeping Safe

This section of *Keeping Safe* extends the ideas and strategies of children learning to trust their own judgement, being able to say no, getting away and telling, to other areas. Drugs and alcohol, AIDS, video nasties, bullies and other worries are concerning many of us. How can we best help children to be alert to the dangers and be aware ourselves, without finally deciding that we should move to a desert island?

One of the most important things we can do is to know what may confront our children and find out as much as possible about them.

The chapters in this section are intended to give an overview, the basic facts as we now know them, and ideas to help. But if drugs, alcohol or AIDS are of particular concern to you, then see 'Where to Get Help' (pp 127-34) and 'Further Information' (pp 171-90) for more in-depth sources of knowledge.

3 DRUGS/SOLVENT AND ALCOHOL ABUSE

As they grow up, most children will find themselves in a situation in which they will have to decide what to do about drugs and alcohol. The choices they make are influenced by pressure from friends, natural curiosity, availability of drugs and alcohol, conflicting values and information, their own personalities, and a variety of other circumstances.

Taking drugs, for example, may have nothing to do with the adults around them – some children drift into drugs even when parental guidance and example has been as good as humanly possible. Others are influenced into taking drugs or using alcohol or smoking by what they see around them. Certainly the use of alcohol and smoking are portrayed by the media as being glamorous and sophisticated. The pressures on young people are enormous.

Yet when we advise our children not to drink or take drugs, we hope that they will listen. However, the old adage that children learn more from what they see than what they are told is relevant here. Adults drink to feel good, to celebrate, to compensate, to toast success, to drown sorrows. Adults take medication and pills to feel good, to lose weight, to sleep, to wake up, to keep going, to dull the pain. The message to children and young people is that we can alter, improve or cover up various aspects of life by taking something: there is no need to feel bad – ever.

But some of the drugs/solvents which will help children to fulfil the promise of eternally feeling good are more foreign and frightening to adults than the 'known' drugs, such as alcohol, cigarettes or pills. Few parents feel confident to deal with the perplexing problems of drug abuse by their children when heroin, cocaine, magic mushrooms, glue sniffing, etc. are involved, sometimes in a deadly mixture, with the more familiar ones, such as alcohol.

WHAT CAN PARENTS DO?

- From the time children are very young, be aware of your own attitude towards drugs and alcohol, especially if there are tranquillisers, alcohol, cigarettes, or seditives freely available in your home.

- Find out about the facts concerning drugs/solvents and alcohol in order to be a reliable source of information for your child. Contact any of the groups listed under the 'Help' section (pp 130–31). They may be able to tell you about local lectures or groups that meet to discuss the problems of drugs. Also get one of the books or the free leaflets listed under 'Resources' at the back of the book. Some of these excellent publications define, illustrate and clearly explain the kinds of drugs currently available.

This doesn't mean that you have to become a 'drug or alcohol expert'. But knowing what kinds of drugs are available, what they look like, how they are used and what they are called means that a question from your child can be answered by you. If children feel they can ask parents and receive reliable information, it may reduce their vulnerability to inaccurate or harmful input from friends or drug pushers.

Keep up to date about the latest drug crazes and issues through media coverage and other sources as this will maintain your credibility with your children.

- Keep an adult perspective. Don't feel it is necessary to be on the same level with your children by using slang and acting cool to prove how aware and young you are. Children need an adult point of view; they have enough of the youth viewpoint from friends and peers.

- Don't be afraid to say that using drugs is wrong and to have rules about drugs and alcohol. If children don't feel strong enough to say no on their own, they can use your rules as an 'out' with their friends – 'My Mum will kill me if I do that.'

- Get together with other parents and agree on curfews, pocket money, use of the car, and any other guidelines which make it harder for young people to say 'everyone else does it'.

- Provide or encourage activities for young people, such as discos and sports.

- Help your child develop the confidence to say no. Talk about ways to get out of situations, such as being at a party where drugs are offered. Discuss what to do if a friend or pusher is bothering your child to try glue sniffing or drugs.

- Find out which parents allow alcohol at parties for children below the legal drinking age and don't allow your child to attend these gatherings.

- Keep communications open. It is important that children feel that you are interested in what they are thinking. Ask their opinions about drugs, but don't turn these talks into a nightly 'Oh no, it's Dad's lecture on drugs' time. Even more importantly, be careful not to hype the whole issue to the point where curiosity is aroused so that young people decide to experiment.

- Depending upon the age of your child, explain the dangers of contracting the HIV virus (see chapter 4 on AIDS) and other diseases such as hepatitis B from contaminated needles. Young children need to be warned about picking up discarded syringes because of the possibility of scratching or accidently stabbing themselves.

- When discussing glue sniffing, be sure to explain as well the dangers of inhaling other volatile chemicals, such as deodorants, hair spray, spray polishes, petrol fumes, etc. Younger children may be particularly vulnerable to experimenting with these substances without realising the consequences.

One way to explain these dangers to children from the time they are quite small is to answer their questions in a matter-of-fact manner. For example:

Daphne was helping her six-year-old granddaughter assemble a model, when the child remarked on how good the glue smelled. The grandmother replied that it did, but that glue could also be quite dangerous, as well as being useful for sticking things together. As her granddaughter was interested and receptive, they talked briefly about the good and bad aspects of glue and then went on to other topics.

By using the natural curiosity and questions of children, we can establish early the kind of communication which will allow for non-emotive discussion of the pros and cons of issues without destroying our relationships with our children.

Possible indicators

Be aware of the signs of drug, solvent and alcohol abuse. The information from the leaflets mentioned under 'Resources' will prove useful, but do not use signs like a check list. As in the case of sexual abuse, there may be other explanations for the symptoms. But it may be cause for concern if your child:

- Has an inexplicable personality change
- Starts keeping peculiar hours
- Becomes secretive, vague or withdrawn
- Has frequently changing moods
- Begins needing large amounts of money which cannot be adequately explained
- Becomes slovenly in habits or dress
- Stops doing school work
- Drops out of favourite activities
- Becomes irritable, withdrawn, aggressive
- Seems to be alternately drowsy or unable to sleep
- Begins lying, stealing
- Becomes paranoid
- Has slurred or slow speech
- Begins to associate with people who seem to condone drugs
- Uses or leaves lying around drug paraphernalia, such as burnt foil, needles, pipes, books on how to use drugs, tablets, capsules, powders, plastic bags

- Smells of drugs, such as cannabis, hashish
- Has glue on clothing
- Develops red eyes, spots around face, red nose, jerky movements

Most of these symptoms can have other causes. A teenager may develop a need for privacy, for making furtive telephone calls or always be in need of more money. But any significant combination of these behaviours and signs, particularly combined with the paraphernalia and new associates, may indicate a possible drug or solvent abuse problem.

In addition to the obvious physical signs of slurred speech, red eyes and the smell of alcohol, some possible indicators of a person becoming an alcoholic are:

- Drinking to escape problems
- Drinking to build self-confidence
- Drinking owing to unhappiness
- Drinking in the morning
- Craving alcohol at a particular time of day
- Drinking alone
- Having the reputation of being a heavy drinker
- Feeling remorseful after drinking
- Experiencing sleep difficulties
- Missing time from school or work
- Losing ambition or efficiency
- Getting into financial difficulties

Many people may occasionally experience some of these problems with alcohol use. However, if a pattern starts to emerge it is a sign that help is needed.

What if you suspect drug/solvent or alcohol abuse?

- Try to be calm and not overreact. It may not be what you think.

- If you don't feel confident to raise the issue with your child, seek advice or support. This can be from your family, GP, or one of the groups listed under 'Help' (pp 130-31).

- Think before you decide to drag your child along to someone to teach them a lesson. What if it isn't what you think and your child is humiliated for no reason?

- After you have had some time to consider, sit down with your child and perhaps one other person and talk about the problem.

- Although you may be angry and frightened, try not to take it out on your child. Being judgemental or saying 'how could you do this to me?' could make matters worse.

- If things become really tense and the discussion is getting out of hand, take a break, make a cup of tea, get some fresh air or anything to temporarily relieve the pressure and restore some calm.

- Don't automatically assume the guilt. It may have nothing to do with you.

- Decide on what course of action you are going to take: will you contact your GP, the police, a self-help group, social services, drug or alcohol counselor or one of the helplines? For information of some of these groups, see pages 130-31.

- In the unlikely event that your child takes an overdose, act immediately to loosen clothing, turn the child on to his or her side to prevent inhalation of vomit, contact the emergency services or your GP, and take to the hospital a sample of whatever drug, solvent or combination your child has used.

As parents we hope that we will never be in a position to have to deal with drug, solvent or alcohol abuse with our children. However, concern about the safety of children in our 'modern' world unfortunately includes the use of these substances as potential dangers. Knowing more about what our children may have to face may prevent experimentation or curiosity turning into tragedy.

4 AIDS

'I'm not going to sleep with my brother any more,' declared my eight-year-old recently.
 'Why not?'

'Because you can die from sleeping with someone.'
 The next day the query was: 'What's ig-rance?' (Which doesn't say much for his reading skills!)
 'Why?'
 ''Cause you can die from that, too.'

These kind of questions are being asked in homes throughout the country as the very necessary campaign to educate us about AIDS (Acquired Immune Deficiency Syndrome) continues.

Some teens are being taught about the problem of

AIDS through schools and youth clubs, others are relying on information leaflets and the media. Most adults are confused and perhaps worried, but may have some understanding of the problem. We are all ignorant to some degree.

What is concerning many people, as well, are the questions being asked by the under twelves. Linking death and AIDS with sex can be frightening, and we should help them understand the differences. Indeed, many parents have not yet explained sex to children, let alone that certain activities connected with it might lead to death.

Most parents feel that it is wrong for children to link the concept of sex with abuse, as it is wrong to link sex with death. It could have potentially harmful effects as they get older and start relationships. Equally, as they do begin to have relationships, we do not want them at risk because they aren't aware of the dangers.

Because most children under the age of eleven are not involved in sexual relationships which could lead them to contacting the HIV virus, unless they are victims of abuse, it seems unnecessary to explicitly explain the consequences of AIDS to them. This is because that they are unlikely to suffer from the consequences of AIDS, as the disease is understood at this point. It is important, though, to answer their questions and address their fears. As on page 78 in discussing drugs, communication about this issue can be low key (see below).

Older children, however, are actively discovering their own sexuality and how that relates to others. They are therefore making decisions which could affect their lives. It is vital that they are given information to protect themselves. A discussion about AIDS might provide an opportunity to introduce them to a range of issues to do with health and well being. For example, abstinence from sex or drugs is one of the most effective ways to dramatically reduce the chances of contracting the HIV virus. However, the reality is that not all young people will follow this advice.

There are several other recommendations about how to be better protected from the HIV virus:

- Avoid sexual relationships entirely
- Have sexual relations with only one partner
- Avoid having sex with people who have multiple partners
- Do not use intravenous drugs (see page 86)
- If you do use intravenous drugs, use a new needle for each injection – never share needles
- Practise safer sex, which includes:
  - using lubricated condoms which include a spermicide
  - avoiding oral-genital contact
  (see page 128 for where to obtain more information)
- Continue to gain accurate information about AIDS and other diseases which may be transmitted by sexual contact (see pages 127–8 for organisations which may prove helpful)

Until there is sufficient and well-researched teaching material available for young children, it might be best simply to respond to their questions and concerns. For example, much of the media coverage has gone right over the heads of most four- and five-year-old kids. Therefore, it may not be desirable or necessary to try to explain the problem to younger children if they don't appear to be interested or expressing concern.

Teachers and parents report that by the age of six or seven, children are beginning to have questions about AIDS. These children are better able to take on some abstract concepts. But as they often understand more than they can articulate, we must help them to talk. Otherwise they might have fears that will come out in other ways.

For example, one child, having seen the advertisements during an AIDS campaign, featuring icebergs, began having nightmares about icebergs and death.

Some children will talk or joke about AIDS with adult vocabularies but no real understanding. For example, children may tell smutty jokes which they do not really understand about condoms and AIDS. These jokes are one way that children express anxiety, so don't become angry or censorious. Find out how much they understand about the subject. Then give them enough information to satisfy their curiosity, but not so much that they are overwhelmed. Curtail your own anxiety or the desire to tell everything.

If a child asks about AIDS, explaining that AIDS is simply one consequence of infection by Human Immunodeficiency Virus (HIV) is probably more than the child needs to know. Although that may be the most correct definition, it may also be far too much information and too confusing. Better to define it as a disease that, at the moment, affects mainly grownups and that they may die from it. However, also explain that it is difficult to 'catch' the germ that causes AIDS so the child won't be worried that the grownups around him or her will die.

Point out, as well, that not that many grownups have died from it in our country so far, compared to the total population. Also explain that there are hundreds of people around the world working to find a cure and that, hopefully, before the child grows up they will be successful.

If your child asks if children get AIDS, the answer is only in exceptional circumstances. You can explain that some children were given blood transfusions before we knew about AIDS and that some of those children have developed the disease. Assure your child that doctors, scientists and others are working very hard to try to help the children and that very few children have it.

Another concern of children is the babies born with the HIV infection. If asked, say that some babies are born to mummies who have AIDS and that sometimes these babies also get AIDS. You might explain that many of the adults with AIDS were using drugs that they took with infected needles and got the disease that way. Since you and your family probably don't use these kinds of drugs, this is another reassuring factor for children.

There is some concern among the medical profession about the dangers of discarded syringes being found by young children. Children should be warned never to pick up syringes because of the possibility that they might stab or scratch themselves. If this should happen, contact your doctor immediately, as children can be given immunisation against hepatitis B. The other worry is that children might contact the HIV virus from discarded needles, but to date there are no reported cases of this happening.

But there is little point in painting a bleak picture to a child who is unlikely at this time to have to deal with AIDS and who is unable to do anything about it anyway. Although you may be quite anxious both about AIDS and about having to answer your child's questions, keep calm and talk in a low-key way. Don't sensationalise or over-react – children may become worried through your own anxiety.

If children ask questions about condoms or anal sex, try to answer. Avoiding the issue just shows that you are anxious, and they will pick up a more inaccurate explanation from the playground. Keep explanations simple and use words that your child will understand.

One parent answered his young daughter's question about a condom by saying that it was something like a little balloon. That was enough information for her, but if children continue to ask more questions then you must decide how much detail to give. Far better to keep answering their questions, though, than to show yourself unwilling to discuss it. Keep going in stages until they have enough information.

Other sensitive questions can be answered in the same manner. Another parent responded to her son's question about anal sex by explaining that it was 'something some grownups do with their private parts and bottoms'. He asked no more questions, much to his mother's relief, but that may not be the way you choose to answer. Perhaps your children know about sex or may demand a more detailed reply. Some parents feel comfortable giving a more accurate definition. That decision must be left to you.

Whatever you decide to do, it often helps to talk to your partner or other adults you know before you are either asked these questions or sit down to explain things to your child. Some adults even practise what they will say beforehand by roleplaying the discussion with another adult. This can prove to be quite useful because it will help you to discover just how much you know about AIDS and it should help you to discuss it in a matter-of-fact way with your child.

Be as calm and reassuring as possible rather than emotive or embarrassed. If your child is old enough, do explain the concept of safer sex. If you don't know how to answer a question, say so and tell the child you will try to find out. Explain that AIDS is something we are just learning about and no one knows all the answers. If you would like more information about the issue of AIDS, contact one of the groups listed under 'Where to Get Help' (see pp 127–8).

The most important message about AIDS to get across to children, however, is that AIDS has nothing to do with the hugs and kisses that they get at home. You may want to say: 'You won't catch anything from our hugs and kisses except some extra love', or something else that is reassuring to them.

AIDS AT SCHOOL

If a child at your child's school has the HIV virus or has developed AIDS, experts say that there is no danger of other children catching the virus during ordinary school activities. There is much more concern that the infected child will be at more risk from childhood diseases, such as chicken pox. Do talk to the headteacher or contact the organisations in the 'Where to Get Help' section.

Some suggestions for children and young people who are attending school and have the virus are made by the British Medical Association in their booklet on AIDS (see page 128):

- Children should not take part in blood experiments, such as in Biology classes

- They should wear plasters on any cuts

- They should not become involved with mixing blood in the 'blood brother/sister' ritual

- None of the children or young people should engage in tattooing or ear piercing owing to the risk of dirty needles

AIDS AND CHILD SEXUAL ABUSE

If your child is abused, you and the child may be worried about the possibility of being infected with the HIV virus. Contact your paediatrician or doctor who will discuss it with you and arrange a test, if this has not already been done. It is unlikely that the child has been infected, but if he or she is concerned, explain that very few children have developed AIDS. Do not, however, dismiss the child's fears; listen and be supportive.

It is very likely that you and your family will need support during this time. If you do not know where to get help, contact one of the organisations listed on pages 127–8 for information, counselling or advice.

5 AMUSEMENT ARCADES

Amusement arcades attract children and young people. They also attract those who may want to harm children. This is an obvious danger which parents need to consider.

However, they represent another worry in that children can be easily enticed into using the hundreds of thousands of video machines available in arcades, cafés, pubs, sports centres, railway stations, and airports. Millions of pounds a year are spent gambling on these machines and it is having an effect on many young people. The National Housing and Town Planning Council conducted a survey which indicated that more than 400,000 young people between the ages of thirteen and sixteen visit amusement arcades at least once a week and a similar number play machines in shops and cafés. Although the voluntary code of practice states that children aged sixteen or younger should not be admitted to amusement arcades, this code is not enforced and it does not apply to other places with machines.

Parents are becoming increasingly concerned about their children being addicted to playing these machines. Some children are using all their dinner money, bus fares and pocket money on the videos, while others are even resorting to theft. There are reports of children missing school and becoming compulsive gamblers. There have been reports of attempted suicides and murders because of debts accrued by young people misusing these machines.

What can be done? Warning young people about the

dangers and being aware of where they go is obvious advice. But the Parents of Young Gamblers organisation (see page 132) advise that should children get into difficulty over money for gambling, parents should not buy them out of trouble, but get them to repay their debts themselves. The problem should be recognised as more than just a 'passing phase'. In fact this behaviour may be the basis for a gambling addiction and even require therapy.

Another suggestion is to try to bring about legislative changes which will help to protect young people. The voluntary code has not been successful; perhaps these machines should be withdrawn from places where children are allowed unlimited access to them.

At the very least, parents need to be aware of the potential problem that these machines can cause some young people and where they can turn for help at the first sign of trouble. See page 132 for more information.

6 PORNOGRAPHIC VIDEOS

Because of the proliferation of video recorders, many more children are being placed in a situation where it is possible to watch pornographic videos. Often adults will say that the children are 'too young to understand' what's happening on the video. But watching these videos is a form of child abuse and children should be protected from it.

Children are being affected by these films. Some teachers of even nursery-aged children are reporting that they have children coming into class too tired to do work and, when questioned, talk about being up late watching these kinds of videos.

Children learn from things they see and hear. Some children are being introduced to the concept of sex through such videos. Equally worrying is the attitudes and behaviour of men and women toward each other in the videos, particularly the violent ones. The message of many of these videos is that sexual violence and degradation is all right.

Also, there is concern that a child may be subjected to additional sexual abuse by the person who is showing the video. If the child then tells, the video can be used as an excuse – 'I might have shown the video, but I never touched the child. He is just talking about what he saw.'

This introduces the idea that perhaps children make false allegations of sexual abuse after seeing pornographic videos. This has not proven to be the case with young children. When a child has been sexually abused, he or she describes it by saying what happened and how the abuse felt or how it looked or tasted. For example, although a child might be able to describe oral sex from seeing a video, the child would not know that 'it hurt, I couldn't breathe' or that 'it was white and sticky' from seeing a video. These disclosures come from the child's experience and are described in the child's words.

Another worry about these videos is the way they are displayed in some video rental shops at a level that young children can easily see the covers. Some parents have protested and been successful in at least getting them relegated to a more inaccessible place, if not having them removed altogether.

Children in most homes do not have access to pornographic videos, but one young mum was horrified when she came early to collect her three-year-old from the child minder's and walked in to find an explicit video on with the children watching. The childminder was unconcerned because she said, 'the children were too young to be bothered'. If your children are in the care of a babysitter, check on the kinds of 'entertainment' that are available. Also, if your older children spend time at friends' houses watching videos, it would be a good idea to find out what is being shown.

7 BULLYING

Bullying is a problem for many children, regardless of their age. In fact, it is probably the single largest worry that children have. I conducted a two-year study which included asking children about being bullied. Approximately thirty-eight per cent of the children in the study had been bullied, some quite severely. It was a concern not only to the children, but to the parents and teachers as well. Thirty per cent of the parents said they were worried about their children being bullied, but only four per cent had tried to do something about it. The majority told their children to fight back, which is advice that most of us have received during childhood.

For many victims, it is not possible to fight back; it sometimes makes the situation worse. The suggestions under 'What Can Be Done?' (see pp 98–102) have worked for some children and studies are continuing into the problem. The age-old attitude that bullying has always gone on so why worry is starting to change. We know that the victims of bullying may become frightened of going to school, have nightmares, feel humiliated, or even become suicidal. In extreme cases, children have sought revenge by killing the bully or the victims have been killed. Although this kind of outcome is rare, it is not rare for children to suffer real torment as a result of being bullied.

Bullying takes many forms. It can be physical, emotional or verbal, or a combination of all of these. It might involve a gang of bullies beating up a child or a group of children refusing to talk to another child. It could mean viciously verbally attacking a child. The bully can be another child or an adult.

What if your child is the bully?

Although most chronic bullies have themselves been bullied or abused in some way, sometimes a child becomes a bully for other reasons. A divorce, the birth of a new baby, boredom, frustration, the death of a loved one and other situations could result in a child taking out his or her problems on another child through bullying. Usually this is a short-term problem, but it causes parents, children and teachers considerable worry.

If you find out your child is being a bully:

- Remain calm

- Try to find out what has happened. Talk to your child, to the teachers and anyone else who might give you information. This could include the playground supervisor, the caretaker, the dinner staff

- If you can find no immediately obvious reason for the

bullying, put aside time to talk with your child to try to uncover what has caused this uncharacteristic behaviour. Your child may not respond at first, but keep trying. Ask questions about friends, home, school. Give the child time to think and reflect – don't turn it into the Spanish Inquisition

- Don't make a mountain out of a molehill. If the situation is not serious, give it time to sort itself out

- If the situation is serious, don't hesitate to get help. Ask the school to get in touch with the educational psychologist or contact your local Child Guidance Centre

Why do children become chronic bullies?

There may be many reasons why some children become bullies and go through life using bullying behaviour. In growing up, these children often:

- Feel insecure
- Feel inadequate
- Feel humiliated
- Are bullied by parents or siblings
- Become the scapegoat in the family
- Are physically, sexually or emotionally abused
- Are under pressure to succeed at all costs
- Are not allowed to show feelings
- Feel that they cannot fit in, that they look odd or feel different to their peers
- Feel no sense of accomplishment

Often a bully is a victim of some sort of abuse or neglect. He or she has been made to feel inadequate, stupid and humiliated. Children who are nurtured and loved can cope with being vulnerable and dependent, and with making mistakes or not doing everything properly. This is a normal part of growing up.

Some children are punished or humiliated for things they cannot help, like accidently wetting the bed, not being hungry when adults decide it is time to eat, spilling a drink, falling over and getting hurt or putting on a jumper back to front. The adults expect impossible things from the child and make it clear that being dependent and vulnerable are not acceptable. Being 'strong' and humiliating others are the acceptable ways to behave – indeed, the only ways to behave if the child is to survive.

The child comes to deny and hate this vulnerable self. It is linked with weakness and being weak is associated with pain. When this child perceives that another child is weak in any way, he or she attacks. But the sad fact is that the bully is really attacking himself – it is self hatred that makes a bully.

Bullies need help, but usually reject any attempt at giving them some. Realistic, firm guidelines and rules may help them to control their reactions and lashing out behaviour. Also trying to help them achieve some success can make a difference. One boy was nurtured by a teacher who helped him to learn skills in woodworking. He began to produce beautiful boxes which the teacher made sure were prominently displayed and admired. The boy found a part of himself that he could like and stopped bullying others. Unfortunately, the 'success' that most bullies achieve is by being a bully and other children need help to cope with the problem.

What can be done?

Children first need to know that there are some situations which might be impossible to deal with – a gang of bullies attacking one child or a bully with a weapon. Since the child's safety is the primary concern, advise that it is not worth getting badly hurt for money or anything else. Sometimes it is better to give the bully what he or she asks for and get away and tell.

Some parents feel it is best to just give as good as you get. If a child reports being bullied, the response is 'hit back or you will continue to be bullied'. While this tactic can work, it places the often smaller, weaker victim in an impossible situation. And bullies are most likely to choose this kind of victim.

There are some children who always seem to be bullied. It would be helpful to examine the child's behaviour to find out if he or she is acting like a victim. Perhaps the child needs to learn to walk in a more confident manner or learn to express feelings of anger and become more self-assertive. It is also important to discover whether something like wearing the 'wrong' type of clothing is making the child a victim of bullying.

One family helped their son by practising walking, which increased his self-confidence. Initially they had the child walking as if frightened, head down and shoulders hunched. They then discussed how it felt inside. 'Scared,' replied the child.

They then had him practising walking with his head held high, taking long strides and looking straight ahead. Asked what it felt like, the boy said, 'Strong'. It was a simple way to begin to help him understand how the bully might be looking at him.

It is best to repeat this kind of exercise over weeks and involve other family members or friends, giving the child lots of praise. It should not be done if it creates tension or if it becomes a form of bullying to the child. Then it would only make the child feel worse.

Since victims of bullying are often timid, the saying no exercise on page 20 is also quite helpful. Expressing anger through the tone of voice can be a confidence booster.

If your child is tied into knots by a difficult situation, such as bullying, help them get the anger out and express those feelings. Drawing and working with plasticine are two good ways to do this. For example, it is therapeutic to make a plasticine model of the bully and act out inner frustrations. This can lead to more open discussion and help you to develop strategies with your child about how to cope and what to do.

Coping might include getting friends to help, if possible, as in the school situation mentioned below. One little girl practised saying no in front of the mirror for a month, learned to walk in a more assertive way and her mother arranged for a friend to walk with her to school. When the bully did approach, the girl looked her right in the eye, said, 'Leave me alone' very loudly and firmly and walked away. The bully started to follow and the girl and her friend turned around and shouted, 'Get away from us'.

In this case, the bully was so startled at being confronted that she left. In another recent case, two eleven-year-old boys were walking home from school when two older youths with knives walked towards them. Since it was not an isolated area and the police station was within sight, the younger boys both yelled a deep, loud yell and ran around the older youths to the police station. They gave an accurate description and the youths were apprehended.

In both of these cases, being with someone else helped the children to cope with the situations. We must make sure that in teaching our children to protect themselves from bullying, that they do not use aggressive tactics inappropriately and end up becoming a bully. Nor should they place themselves at risk of greater harm, if at all possible. In the case of the youths with knives, the boys felt they would be badly hurt if they allowed the youths to get close enough to them. The boys took the decision to get out of the situation fast because they knew they could get help. They might not have done the same thing had there been no one around to help. At least both groups of children had options and were not left vulnerable because of lack of information.

It is particularly difficult when a child has been part of a group that turns and starts to bully him or her. Sometimes it is one of those temporary phases where one or another of the group is in or out of favour. Other times it becomes a real vendetta, usually led by one of the old gang. When this happens, the choice is to find a new group, which is often very difficult, or to try to stop the victimisation and get back into the group.

One mum successfully helped her son to break the cycle by inviting a couple of the boys' families around for a barbeque. It broke the group's desire to bully this boy. It also eventually led to a parent's group which worked on the general problem of bullying in the neighbourhood. Part of their strategy was to say to their children that it was all right to tell if they were being bullied – that it is not telling tales.

But if children tell, adults must be prepared to try to help, as these parents did. Bullying then becomes unacceptable behaviour within the community and the children feel comfortable supporting one another.

If this kind of community cooperation isn't possible, try asking over one or two of the group that your child wants to become friends with again. Ensure that there is a lot to do and that they have a good time, which will make it much more difficult for the children to want to bully your child. Gradually increase the size of the group so that your home becomes a focal point and somewhere that the children want to go. This is extra work, but it is usually worth it. Better to spend your energy creating a positive situation than trying to pick up the pieces of a bullied child.

One of the best ways to address bullying is by enlisting the teacher, the children and parents in the school to make the prevention of bullying a priority. For example, this problem is one dealt with in the Kidscape programme and some schools have reported that bullying has stopped. This happened because the children learned that bullying was cowardly, they stuck together and the bully was not only left without victims, but sometimes became a positive member of the group.

These approaches work best when started at the primary level, but teenage bullying can be combated with education and peer pressure as well.

Although bullying is not always easy to stop, it is certainly worth trying to change the behaviour of chronic bullies because of the damage done both to themselves and their victims. The long-term effects of chronic bullying are beginning to be studied.

At the University of Illinois in the U.S., a twenty-year study of bullies has shown that children who were chronic bullies from a young age were much more likely as adults to be violent, to have committed crimes, to have battered their wives and children, and to have difficulty with relationships, than children who were not bullies.

Although it might not have only been the bullying that caused these problems, it is evident that bullying can and does cause considerable misery. By helping our children develop strategies to cope with the problems now, we may be helping to alleviate more difficult problems in the future.

8 OTHER TIPS FOR SAFETY

WHEN TO GIVE INDEPENDENCE

Parents are always concerned about when first to allow children to venture out in pairs or alone. One mother stated that she would permit her children to be independent 'next year'. She said the only problem was that when next year came, it was always too soon.

Having surveyed 4,000 parents over a two-year period about this question of independence, the only single thing that everyone agreed on was that the maturity of the child and not the age determined the degree of independence. Also, where the family lived and the distances children were going to travel were important factors. However, there was a certain consensus about the age which most parents:

- Started allowing children to cross local roads. Having reached the maturity level of nine years was the agreed mean age

- Allowed children to go to the cinema or shopping. With a friend or sibling, the average age was twelve

- Permitted children to use public transport for local journeys in daylight hours. It was generally agreed that eleven or twelve was a reasonable age for this

- Allowed young people out on their own or with a friend during evening hours before eleven p.m. The parents were most concerned about this, but most thought that age fifteen or sixteen was all right

All the parents questioned said that they worried constantly when first giving children independence and continued to worry at least a little no matter how old their children were. One father said that he never slept soundly until his whole brood was in, though the eldest was now twenty-two.

Although it is one of the most difficult tasks for a parent, we must help our children towards being independent. But teaching them strategies for helping themselves should make the task a little easier.

TIPS ON PUBLIC PLACES

Children and young people need to be aware of safety strategies to use in a variety of situations.

Lifts and stairways

Talk with children and teenagers about what they should do if they feel uncomfortable about either using the stairs or a lift if there are people around who worry them. An eight-year-old girl was recently sexually assaulted in a lift when a man got into the lift and stopped it between floors. In this case, the child did exactly as she was told because there was no chance of escape or of attracting anyone's attention by yelling. She survived the attack, though was emotionally damaged. Later she recounted how she had thought of getting out when the man got into the lift, but didn't want to appear rude.

Although it may take longer to get to their destination, children and teens should always feel they can get out of a lift should they feel at all concerned. Explain that they can either walk out and wait for the lift to return, or get out on another floor if it is safe to do so. The same applies to using the stairs – better to wait a few minutes or even longer, if there is a person or a group of people who make you feel unsafe. By discussing it, you can help children plan what to do if the situation arises.

Public toilets

If possible, always go with your child when using a public toilet. As they grow older, it becomes problematic. For example, by the age of eight most boys refuse to go into the women's toilet. This leaves mothers outside shouting, 'Are you all right?' and little boys saying, 'I can take care of myself'. The same applies to fathers taking care of daughters. As parents we are left with no choice and we should encourage children to build up their self-confidence through incidents like this.

But we must also talk with children about what to do if they are accosted in a public toilet. At a meeting about children's safety, one mother told how her nine-year-old son had gone to use the toilet in a very well-known eating place which welcomes children. He came out looking pale and agitated. A man had fondled him and the boy had been too frightened even to run. The mother had not thought about warning her son and certainly did not consider this kind of incident possible in such a place.

Had the boy known that he should have left when the man started talking about showing him a surprise, the assault might not have happened. It is planning strategies with children – 'What would you do if?' type questions – and giving children permission to leave situations, which provide the basis of keeping safe.

Public transport

If children and teenagers are travelling on trains or the underground, tell them always to get into carriages where there are other people. If possible, they should travel in the carriage with the guard. Also explain that they should change carriages if they find themselves alone, if there is just one other person or a gang that seems to be together in the carriage.

Make sure that they know about how and when to use the emergency handle or cord. A teenage boy was beaten by a gang while travelling in a carriage alone. He considered pulling the emergency cord, but thought he would automatically have to pay the fine. Another child in a similar situation was too short to reach the handle and did not think to stand on the seat. One important point to remember when travelling on the underground is to pull the emergency handle when the train is in the station, rather than when it is moving.

When travelling on buses, sit downstairs near the conductor or driver. When travelling by taxi, try always to use licensed taxis. Ask the driver either to escort you or wait until you are in your flat or house. When leaving any form of transport, make sure that you are not being followed. If you feel uncomfortable, do not leave. Better to stay on for one more stop, which might be safer than getting off. Tell children or teens that they can always ring you to collect them or take a taxi which you will pay for when they arrive.

A good habit to instil in children from the time they start going out on their own is always to carry enough money for a return journey home and never spend it on anything else.

These same kind of strategies apply to going to the cinema, to swimming baths, to playgrounds and parks, to dances, to clubs, and to any other place where children or young people may find themselves. Of course it is best always to accompany young children, never to leave them alone in cars or at home and generally to ensure their safety. But as children grow, they must develop ways to cope with being on their own. Hopefully they will never have to use the strategies mentioned above, but at least we can give them some options.

TELEPHONE TIPS

Children should be taught how to use the telephone as it can be a lifeline to them in case of emergency. Be sure that your children know how to use dial, push button and pay telephones.

Do *not* teach children to answer the telephone by repeating their name and telephone number. Many obscene telephone callers continue to ring back after being told the number they have reached. Since these callers often seem to dial at random, it is best not to give them a way to ring back.

Help children and teenagers practise making an emergency call. Explain that you do not need money to call from a pay telephone, if you dial 999 or 100. It is also important for children to know that they can make a reverse charge call and how to do it.

It is helpful to roleplay using a telephone, because during an actual emergency it is difficult to remember what to do if you've only been told and have never done it. In fact, write your telephone number and address in large print by the telephone as people often forget this vital information when making a call under stress.

Explain that the operator will want to know your telephone number and which service you need – fire, police or ambulance. The service will also ask for your name, address and the location of the emergency. Depending upon the age of your child, this is probably the only circumstance under which it is all right to give out a name, address and number over the telephone.

Make your child pretend to dial 999 to report a fire. Acting as the operator, say:

Adult: 'Emergency, what is your number?'

Child: '800 6543'

Adult: 'Which service do you want?'

Child: 'Fire'

Adult: 'Fire Service, what is your number?'

Child: '800 6543'

Adult: 'Your name?'

Child: 'John Smith'

Adult: 'Where are you calling from?'

Child: '42 Meadow Grove'

Adult: 'What is the emergency?'

Child: 'The house next door is on fire'

Practise several times over a week, using different services. After the child is comfortable with the idea, try making it a surprise game to ensure that your child automatically knows what to do. You might set a problem such as: 'There's been an accident involving a car and a motorbike. You're the only witness. What do you do?' Reward the correct responses. As emergencies arise unexpectedly, it is a good idea to be able to respond quickly.

The exchange with the emergency services usually take less than a minute, although it may seem quite time consuming. Impress on children that they should try to get an adult to make emergency telephone calls, if possible and that *no one* should make one unless there really is an emergency.

Obscene calls

Explain that some people don't use the telephone correctly and it is possible that a person could ring up and say something rude or even just breathe in a funny way. Some suggested advice to your child might be:

Hang up immediately. What the caller wants you to do is to react to what is being said and he/she will probably not ring again if there is no reaction. If the person rings back and there is no one home to help you deal with the situation, try to ring for help from a grownup. This can be your parents, grandparents or a neighbour. If this is not possible, take the telephone off the hook until an adult gets home and tell immediately what happened.

Getting an obscene telephone call can be a frightening

experience for anyone. Acknowledge that it is frightening and encourage the child to talk about his or her feelings. Try not to just dismiss a child's questions such as 'Will that person come and find me?'. This is a real worry and saying 'Of course not' might not help. One way to deal with this kind of question is: 'You must be worried about that. What did he say would happen?'

Allow the child to respond and talk through some of his or her concerns. Explain that the people who make these kind of telephone calls have problems, but that they hide at home and do not come after people. Assure the child that the person cannot see him or her and does not know where you live. If your child has bad dreams after such a call, see page 36.

If the calls persist, contact the police or have your calls intercepted by the operator. In one case, the child was more reassured by the arrival of the police than anything her mum had said. The reality that it is difficult to apprehend the culprit was not important – the police officer made the child feel more protected and she felt that something was being done.

A further alternative is to keep a whistle next to the telephone and after ensuring that it is the obscene caller, blast away. Finally, have your number changed if the calls cannot be stopped in any other way. (See page 133.)

Taking messages

If your children answer the telephone when at home alone, explain that they should never admit to being alone (also see 'Babysitting'). Practise answers such as 'My Mum is in the bath. If you will leave your number, she will ring you back', or 'My Dad is having a nap, may I take a message please?' The friends of one child's mum were amazed at the number of baths she seemed to take, so do vary the message from time to time.

ChildLine/Samaritans and other helplines

The number of children and young people who feel they need to talk about a wide range of issues has become apparent from how many of them are calling ChildLine, the Samaritans and other telephone services. Although we may feel that it is preferable for children and teens to talk about their concerns with someone they know, this is not always possible. In some cases, where a child is being beaten or otherwise abused at home, the child may feel it is impossible to tell anyone else.

Alternatively, a child may just want to discuss a problem, such as being pressured to take drugs or being bullied, with someone outside the family. These telephone listening services can provide a valuable source of advice and comfort to some children and young people. The long and successful history of the Samaritans with adults and young people attests to this.

The lines can also act as an interim step in assisting children to seek help in abusive situations. ChildLine and Incest Crisis Line report that the most frequent concerns of children are about physical and sexual abuse.

Although we want our children to talk with us, it is a good idea to make them aware that they have the option of seeking help from other members of the family, from friends and from organisations such as the Samaritans and ChildLine. Calls to ChildLine, which is national, are free and The Samaritans have local numbers. See the 'Where To Get Help' section for numbers.

Chatlines/'message lines'

Many parents are becoming concerned about the advent of telephone chatlines, which young people can ring to talk with or listen to several other callers. The worries are about who might be listening in, and the exchange of telephone numbers and addresses over the lines. This clearly creates a potential danger for the unwary caller, as well as a sometimes startling telephone bill for the parents.

The message lines are for people to ring in to listen to pre-recorded messages. Unfortunately, some of the lines carry quite unsavoury messages and there is no way of knowing the age of the callers. Parents are not all-knowing, but we do need to be aware that these 'services' may be available to our children. In fact, some parents have formed action groups in an attempt to stop these type of telephone lines.

TIPS ON BABYSITTERS

Finding a babysitter is not always easy, but parents need to carefully consider any person who is left in charge of their children. Unfortunately, molesters do sometimes advertise themselves as babysitters as it is an excellent way to make sure that children are on their own. Therefore, when choosing a babysitter try to:

- Find a trusted family member or friend with whom you and your child feel comfortable and happy

- Find babysitters who have been recommended by friends, but do check references

- Make arrangements with friends to babysit for each other's children

- If you must use a stranger, check several references

- Be very aware of your child's reaction when you say that the babysitter is coming. One little girl cried and cried whenever she was left with the lodger. Her mum thought it was temper, though she wasn't like that with anyone else. The child was scolded for her behaviour. The lodger, a trusted individual, abused her over a two-year period

- Ring home to check and ask to speak to your child. This is another situation in which a code word might be useful so that the child could signal concern. Explain to your child that you will come home if he or she used the code word, but that it should be used *only* if the child feels in danger. Otherwise, you could end up coming home just because the TV is broken!

- Be concerned if the babysitter makes excuses so that you cannot talk with your child

- Be wary of men who always make it a point to volunteer to sit and seem much more interested in your child's friendship than your own. These same people may continually offer to take the children out to give you a break. This does not mean to mistrust all men or not to let them babysit! However, this particular pattern of only being interested in children could be a warning sign

- Always provide the babysitter with emergency telephone numbers and other contacts. If you don't have a telephone, make sure that the sitter knows where to find the nearest one

TIPS FOR TEENAGERS WHEN LOOKING FOR PART-TIME JOBS

When deciding on a job, working a paper round or babysitting for anyone, it is important to be aware of who you are working for and what to do in emergencies:

- Don't answer adverts that ask for sitters or other casual jobs when on your own. One fifteen-year-old recently responded to a card in the newsagents and arranged to meet the 'father' at a place which turned out to be a derelict house. She was raped and beaten. The offender was not found

- Accept jobs through friends, if possible, and find out about the people in advance. Go along with your friend or a parent to meet the employer before accepting the position

- Be sure that your parents know where you are and how to contact you

- Find out about how you will get to the job and home. If it is late, arrange a ride with your parents or the child's parents if babysitting

- If the person who is supposed to give you a lift is drunk, under no circumstances go with them. Phone your parents, a friend or a taxi. A job is not worth your life

- If babysitting, know where to contact the children's parents

- Don't let anyone know that you are alone, whatever the job. If someone rings to talk to your employers, just say they aren't available at the moment. Make up an excuse like 'They are taking stock, can I take your number?' or 'The children's father is resting at the moment, can I get him to return your call?'

- If something happens which frightens you, do not hesitate to ring for help, either from your parents or from the police

- If babysitting, do not answer the door or allow the children to unless you have previous arrangements with someone who is coming with the knowledge of the parents

- Be aware of how to make an emergency telephone call (see pp 107–9)

- Find out the quickest ways out of your place of employment in case of fire or other emergencies. If baby-sitting, plan in advance how you would get the children out with you

- If you do a paper round, be aware if someone seems to be acting suspiciously or appears to be following you. If you have even the slightest doubt, knock on the door of one of your customers or go into the nearest shop. It does not matter what time it is, early morning or late at night, get someone's attention

- If you need urgent help or are frightened for your safety in whatever job you are doing, do not be afraid to make a fuss or break a window to call attention to the situation

- Always report anything like being followed, flashed at or seeing someone who appears to be in difficulty, no matter how insignificant it may seem to you. Reporting an incident could alert the police to a real danger and might even save a life. In many of the reports of children and young people who have gone missing, often witnesses have come forward after the event to tell of suspicious people who were around just before the child disappeared. By being alert and telling someone, you might be able to help prevent a child being harmed

- Also be aware of and report any incident relating to property, like a smashed window, which could be a sign of vandalism or burglary. But do not investigate it or you might be placing yourself at risk

Conclusion

9 DOES PREVENTION WORK?

The positive message of this book is that parents and adults who care about children and young people do have ways of helping them learn how to stay safe. Despite the disturbing facts about sexual abuse; the worries about drug, alcohol and solvent abuse; the concern about bullying and other problems, there are many reported incidents of the effectiveness of teaching prevention. Of course, it is not possible to know if children would have reacted in the following ways without being taught. However, the children reported that they knew what to do because they had thought about and practised ways to keep safe.

These are just a few of the hundreds of cases reported to Kidscape:

- Twelve-year-old Jane and her nine-year-old brother, Edward, were walking through a large common area when two teenage bullies tried to attack them. Both children started shouting for help, kicked the attackers and made a general commotion. The teenagers ran away and the children went for help, contacting their parents who telephoned the police. The children were both shaken, but unhurt.

- One nine-year-old girl was in a community centre toilet when a stranger tried to grab her. She responded with a loud yell and kicked him hard on the shin. This startled him long enough for her to run out and get help. The man fled with staff in pursuit, but got away. The child was safe.

- A teenager was at a party when alcohol and drugs were offered. There was strong pressure to join in, but the girlexcused herself to 'go to the loo'. She then telephoned her parents and arranged for them to collect her.

- After a workshop, a seven-year-old boy revealed that a neighbour had touched him in his private parts the previous week. The child had been told that this was a 'special secret' not to be told to anyone. The parents were contacted, the family given supportive help and the offender was arrested. The child was saved from further molestation and seems to be recovering because of the way in which the situation was handled. He was believed, told that it was not his fault and praised for telling.

- A fifteen-year-old boy, Tony, was at a party with friends when a group of older boys gatecrashed. They turned over the furniture, broke glasses and started becoming abusive to the girls. The teenagers were frightened and there were no adults around. Tony edged away and left the party by a back entrance, went to the nearest telephone and rang for the police. He was scared, but later said that discussing 'What If?' situations at home had helped him remain calm and plan what to do.

- Three weeks after a workshop, an eight-year-old girl told her teacher that her fifteen-year-old brother was coming into the bathroom while she was bathing and trying to touch her. The girl told him to leave her alone and with the help of the teacher told her mother. The abuse was stopped before it started and the boy received counselling.

- Twelve-year-old Emily was offered a drug by one of the older students at her school. She felt too frightened to say no because she was on her own and the older student threatened her. Emily pretended to go along and accept the drug. She even promised not to tell because she was worried about being hit. As soon as she got away, she told the school nurse. Emily understood that her safety was worth the pretence and that she was not bound by her promise.

- A fourteen-year-old girl told her mother that her stepfather was coming into her bedroom at night and trying to kiss and fondle her. Although at first the mother did not believe her, the school social worker helped the mother to understand that the girl was telling the truth. The family received help from the social services.

- Eleven-year-old Sharon was walking home after school when a man in a car called to her. She kept her distance and ran into a shop. She noted the kind of car and was able to give a description of it and the man to the police.

- A teenage girl had been babysitting. When the father of the children offered to take her home, she was quite worried because he had obviously had too much to drink. She politely told him that she had rung her parents earlier in the evening and they were planning on collecting her (not true). The man insisted that he would drive her, so the girl asked to ring her parents to explain. She and her parents had a prearranged code to indicate trouble. The girl used the code and because they had previously discussed various possible difficulties, the parents were able to figure out the problem. They told her not to leave under any circumstances and came over immediately.

- A ten-year-old boy was approached by a gym instructor who tried to fondle him. He said no and told his parents. Two other cases were uncovered and the police were called in.

- A babysitter offered a six-year-old child a sweet to take off his clothes and play 'secret' games. The child put himself to bed and told his parents when they came home.

- A young teenage girl met an older boy at a disco. He bought her drinks and offered to take her home to 'meet his parents'. She felt very grownup and agreed to go with him. He seemed very nice, though he was in her words, 'a little drunk'. When they got to his flat, his parents weren't there and she started to get worried. He began kissing her and acting aggressively. Although she was frightened, she acted calmly and started talking in a reassuring and friendly way. She asked for a drink and when the boy went into the kitchen, she ran out of the front door and knocked loudly on the door of another flat on the floor below. Luckily, the people answered and she was able to ring for help.

It is unrealistic to think that children can always keep themselves safe, but in these cases the children were able to say no and get help. We will never know whether these and the other children we have heard about would have kept safe anyway. How do you assess what might have happened but didn't? But it does seem that learning preventive techniques helps children know what to do in dangerous situations, makes them more confident and less vulnerable.

By educating children about practical ways of avoiding dangerous situations and teaching them that it is all right to say no, to get away, to seek adult help and not to keep bad secrets, we are permitting them to use their judgement to protect themselves.

All children have the right to be safe. It is the responsibility of adults to protect this right.

10 WHERE TO GET HELP

The decision about getting outside help must be made according to the circumstances. Parents or other interested adults can contact either the local social services, a GP or the police. (Please note that if local authorities receive information suggesting that there are grounds for bringing care proceedings in respect of a child or young person, they have a statutory duty to investigate the case unless they consider it unnecessary.) Your church or local religious organisation may also be helpful. In addition, there are several organisations listed below that offer help and advice. If you want to know the policy of the help organisation about reporting, ask before you proceed.

ABUSE

United Kingdom

ChildLine. Freepost 1111 (no stamp needed), London EC4 4BB.
0800 1111
24 hour charge-free telephone counselling and advice service for children in trouble or danger.

Child Helpline. (0742) 886886.
Offers telephone advice and support for children around the Sheffield area who are victims of abuse.

Family Contact Line. (061) 941 4066, 10am to 10pm.
Provides a telephone listening service to families, and nursery facilities.

Family Network. c/o National Children's Home, 85 Highbury Park, London N5 1UD.
Scotland: (041) 221 6722; Wales: (0222) 29461; north of England: (061) 236 9873; south of England: (0582) 422751.
Provides help for children and families with problems. There is a telephone counselling service.

Incest Crisis Line. Richard: (01) 422 5100; Shirley: (01) 890 4732. 24 hour service.
A support group for anyone involved in an incestuous relationship, either past or present.

In Support of Sexually Abused Children. Angela Rivera, PO Box 526, London NW6 1SU, (01) 202 3024.
Offers support for sexually abused children and their parents.

Linkline. (01) 645 0505
Linkline is under the umbrella of OPUS. It is a 24 hour ansaphone for distress calls which gives numbers of groups on call when the office is unattended.

Mothers of Abused Children. Chris Strickland, (0965) 31432, Cumbria.
Support offered for mothers of sexually abused children.

National Society for the Prevention of Cruelty to Children. Head Office, 64–74 Saffron Hill, London EC1N 8RS, (01) 242 1626.
The Society operates in England, Northern Ireland and Wales. See directory for local branches.
The NSPCC aims to prevent child abuse in all forms and to give practical help to families with children at risk.

Organisation for Parents Under Stress (OPUS). 106 Godstone Road, Whyteleafe, Surrey CR3 0EB, (01) 645 0469.
OPUS has a network of thirty self-help groups for parents under stress to prevent child abuse and maltreatment of infants and young children.

Parents Against Injustice (PAIN). 'Conifers', 2 Pledgdon Green, Nr. Henham, Bishop's Stortford, Herts, (0279) 850545.
Gives advice to parents who feel they have been wrongly accused of abusing their children.

Parents Anonymous. 6 Manor Gardens, London N7 6LA, (01) 263 8918, 6pm to 6am.
Parents Anonymous offers help to parents who are tempted to abuse their children and to those who have already done so. There are meetings and a telephone counselling and visiting service for parents by trained volunteer parents.

Rape Crisis Centres. For information on local branches, telephone (01) 837 1600 or write to PO Box 69, London WC1 9NJ.

Royal Scottish Society for the Prevention of Cruelty to Children. Melville House, 41 Polwarth Terrace, Edinburgh EH11 1NU, (031) 337 8539/8530.

Samaritans. See directory for local numbers.
Samaritans are trained volunteers who talk with people about problems of depression and suicide.

Touchline. (0532) 457777
9.30am to 9.30pm, Mon–Fri. Telephone listening service for anyone who has been abused. Located in the Leeds area.

Woman's Therapy Centre. 6 Manor Gardens, London N7 6LA, (01) 263 6200.
Send a large SAE for list of groups and activities.

Irish Republic

Irish Society for the Prevention of Cruelty to Children. 20 Molesworth Street, Dublin 2, Irish Republic, (0001) 760423/4/5.

Australia

Adelaide: Crisis Care, (08) 272 1222   24 hours

Brisbane: Crisis Care, (07) 224 6855   24 hours

Canberra: Children's Services, (062) 462625
9am to 5pm

Darwin: Department for Community Development, (089) 814 733

Hobart: Department for Community
Welfare, Crisis Intervention, (002) 302529   24 hours

Melbourne: Protective Services
for Children, (03) 309 5700   9am to 5pm

Perth: Crisis Care, (09) 321 4144 or
(008) 199 008 (toll free)   24 hours

Sydney: Child Protection and Family Crisis,
(02) 818 5555   24 hours
2UE Kids Careline, (02) 929 7799
9am to 5pm, Mon–Fri

You can also contact through your local directory:
the Police
Lifeline
Rape Crisis Centres

New Zealand

Auckland: Help, Auckland 399 185   24 hours

AIDS

Your GP or paedetrician should be able to give you advice and can arrange for testing, if necessary.

For free leaflets and booklets, contact your local health education unit, which is listed in the directory under the name of your Health Authority.

To obtain a copy of AIDS, What Everyone Needs to Know, write to:
Dept A, P.O. Box 100, Milton Keynes MK1 1TX.

To obtain a copy of the British Medical Association's seventy page illustrated guide entitled AIDS and You, send £1.95 to:
British Medical Association. Tavistock Square, London WC1H 9JP.

You can also contact:

Health Call. 0898 600 699, gives recorded general information on AIDS.
0898 600 900, gives recorded specific information on AIDS.

The Haemophilia Society. 123 Westminster Bridge Road, London SE1 7HR, (01) 405 1010.
The Society will offer advice to people with haemophilia or to the parents of haemophilic children.

Healthline Telephone Service. (01) 981 2717, (01) 980 7222 or from outside London, dial (0345) 581151 and your call will be charged at local rates.
The Healthline gives recorded information and advice about AIDS, safer sex, drug abuse and blood transfusions. 24 hour service.

Terrence Higgins Trust. BM/AIDS, London WC1N 3XX. (01) 833 2971 Monday to Friday 7pm to 10pm, Saturday/Sunday 3pm to 10pm
Offers help and counselling to people with HIV virus or AIDS.

ALCOHOL

For help with dealing with alcohol abuse, contact:

Al-Anon/Al-Teen. 61 Great Dover Street, London SE1 4YF, (01) 403 0888.

For family, friends and children who have a relative affected by drinking problems.

Alcoholics Anonymous. PO Box 1, Stonebow House, Stonebow, York YO1 2NJ.

Alcohol Counselling Service (ACS). 34 Electric Lane, London SW9 8JJ, (01) 737 3579/3570.

ANOREXIA/BULMINIA

Anorexia and Bulminia Nervosa Association. Tottenham Women's Health Centre, Annexe C, Tottenham Town Hall, London N5 4RX.

Anorexia Aid. The Priory Centre, 11 Priory Road, High Wycombe, Bucks HP13 6SL.

Anorexia Family Aid and National Information Centre. Sackville Place, 44/48 Magdalen Street, Norwich, Norfold NR3 1JE.

BEREAVEMENT

Bereaved Parents Helpline, 6 Canons Gate, Harlow, Essex, 0279 412745.
Offers support to parents by telephone and by making visits locally.

Compassionate Friends. 6 Denmark Street, Bristol, BS1 5DQ, 0272 292778.
Offers friendship to parents whose children have died through accident, illness, murder or suicide. Local groups throughout the country.

CONTRACEPTION

For advice on contraception, pregnancy, or abortion, contact:

The British Pregnancy Advisory Service. 7 Belgrave Road, London SW1V 1QB, (01) 222 0985.

Brook Advisory Centres (for young people). Head Office, 153a East Street, London SE17 2SD, (01) 708 1234.

Family Planning Association. 27 Mortimer Street, London W1N 7RJ, (01) 636 7866.

COUNSELLING

These organisations offer counselling on family and other problems:

Family Network Services. c/o National Children's Home, Stephenson Hall, 85c Highbury Park, London N5 1UD.

Birmingham: (021) 440 5970	Luton: (052) 422751
Cardiff: (0222) 29461	Maidstone: (0622) 56677
Glasgow: (041) 221 6722	Manchester: (061) 236 9873
Glenrothes: (0592) 759651	Norwich: (0603) 660679
Gloucester: (0452) 24019	Preston: (0772) 24006
Leeds: (0532) 456456	Swansea: (0792) 292798
London: (01) 514 1177	Taunton: (0823) 73191

National Association of Young People's Counselling and Advisory Service (for young people). 17-23 Albion Street, Leicester LE1 6GD, (0533) 554775.

DRUGS

Doctors, Social Services, Police, and Citizens Advice Bureaus should be able to advise about local services.

For information about drug advice centres, dial 100 and ask for Freefone 'Drug Problems'.

Leaflets about drugs are available from:

Dept DM, DHSS Leaflets Unit, PO Box 21, Stanmore, Middlesex HA7 1AY.

- What every parent should know about drugs (DM 1)
- Drugs: what parents can do (DM2)
- Drug misuse: A basic briefing (DM 3)
- Drugs, What You Can Do as a Parent (DM4)

The Department of Education and Science and Welsh Office also produce leaflets and booklets about drugs available in English and Welsh from:

Welsh Office. Information Division, Cathays Park, Cardiff CF1 3NQ.

To obtain a leaflet on Solvent Abuse:

Solvent Abuse. Dept. M50, 13–39 Standard Road, London NW10.

- What to do about glue-sniffing

Standing Conference on Drug Abuse (SCODA). Kingsbury House, 1–4 Hatton Place, Hatton Garden, London EC1N 8ND, (01) 430 2341.
Will supply a list of local services available throughout the country.

Families Anonymous. 88 Caledonian Road, London N7 9DN, (01) 731 8060.
Provide information about self-help groups for concerned parents.

DRUGS EDUCATION

Teachers Advisory Counsel on Alcohol and Drug Education (TACADE). 2 Mount Street, Manchester M2 SN9.
Provides education and training materials for the formal education system. Write for a full list of materials.

The Society for the Prevention of Solvent Abuse (RE-SOLV). St. Mary's Chambers, 19 Station Road, Stone,

Staffordshire ST15 8JP, (0785) 817885, (0785) 46097.
RE-SOLV produces teaching programmes to help encourage young people to resist experimentation. Has videos and books available. For a full list of resources, send a large SAE.

GAMBLING

Parents of Young Gamblers. Memorial School, Mount Street, Taunton, Somerset TA1 3QB, (0823) 256936.

Gamblers Anonymous. 17–23 Blantyre Street, London SW10 0DT, (01) 352 3060.
Contact either of the above organisations for help and advice about gambling problems.

LEGAL ADVICE

The Children's Legal Centre. 20 Compton Terrace, London N1 2UN, (01) 359 6251.
Gives advice about law and policy affecting children and young people in England and Wales.

Citizen's Advice Bureau.
Will give you details of services available and advice about how to get help. Listed in your local directory.

RUNAWAYS

In addition to the police, contact the Salvation Army for help and advice if your child has run away.

The Central London Teenage Project. c/o The Church of England Children's Society, Edward Rudolf House, Margery Street, London WC1X 0JL, (01) 837 4299.
They have a 'Safe House' for runaways and will pass on messages. They will not, however, give the runaway's location.

SELF-DEFENCE

Contact your library or your local council for information about self-defence classes in your area.

The Metropolitan Special Constabulary. New Scotland Yard, London SW1H 0BG.

The Self-Defence Project. Women's Education Resource Centre, Princeton Street, London WC1R 4BH, (01) 242 6807.

The Suzy Lamplugh Trust. 14 East Sheen Avenue, London SW14 8AS, (01) 876 1839.
The trust has produced a video for those who work with the public and may find themselves in a dangerous situation. The video explains how to recognise and try to talk your way out of danger or what to do if you have to defend yourself. £30 from Citizens Advice Bureaus or contact the Trust.

TELEPHONES

'Nuisance Callers': a leaflet giving guidance on dealing with abusive or nuisance telephone calls. Available free from British Telecom Customer Service.

TRANQUILISERS

Come Off It. 61 Holly Avenue, Jesmond, Newcastle-upon-Tyne, NE6 5EA, (091) 281 1004.

Life Without Tranquilisers. Lynmouth, Devon, EX35 6EE. Send SAE for information and advise about problems caused by tranquilisers or sleeping tables.

Tranquiliser Recovery and New Existence (TRANX). 17 Peel Road, Harrow, Middlesex, HA1 2EZ, (01) 427 2065 and (01) 427 2827.

VICTIM SUPPORT

Victim Support Scheme. Head Office, 17A Electric Lane, London SW9 8LA, (01) 326 1084.
A nationwide network of support groups offering practical help to victims of violence and crime. You can find out about your local branch by contacting the above office.

APPENDIX I

'WHAT IF?' QUESTIONS

The following 'What if?' questions are ways to continue conversations with your children and teenagers about safety issues. Obviously, you will need to decide which questions to raise, depending upon the age and maturity level of your children. Discussing and thinking about what to do is more valuable than being told the 'right' answer. In some situations, there are no right answers. Take care not to overdo them; my eldest son declared 'no more "what ifs?", mum, please!' Nonetheless, we must continue to discuss these subjects until keeping safe becomes second nature.

A mother rang to say that her eleven-year-old son was on his way home from school, when he was confronted by a stranger who tried to pull him into a car. He yelled and ran, went to the police station and gave a description of the car and the man. When he was questioned, the boy said that he knew what to do because he'd been 'kidscaped'. His mother said that she was delighted, but also wanted us to know that her son had professed extreme boredom with the whole topic of safety whenever she brought it up. After the incident, however, he wanted us to know that he 'really wasn't bored and that the "What if?" questions had helped'.

Having children decide on their own questions in groups has been used very successfully in many classrooms. Some families made 'what if?' into a game. Use this section to continue the process of getting children and young people to think for themselves.

'WHAT IF?' QUESTIONS TO ASK YOUR CHILDREN

What if . . .

- you were being bullied by someone at school who had made you promise not to tell?

- you saw a friend steal something from a shop?

- a friend of yours told you a secret which made you feel unsafe and made you promise not to tell?

- your mum asked you to keep your brother's birthday present a secret?

- you were on your way home and you were being followed? You are in a street with only houses and no shops. You do not know anyone who lives around there?

- you are staying with a babysitter and the doorbell rings? The sitter tells you to answer it?

- you notice a fire in the kitchen while dad has just popped out to the papershop?

Keeping Safe, © Michele Elliott 1985, 1986, 1988

- you see someone you don't know steal something from a shop?

- you are grabbed by someone and pulled into a car? The person has you in the front seat of the car and tells you not to do anything?

- you are in the toilet at a restaurant and a person shows you their private parts and offers you a sweet 'not to tell'?

- a grownup told you to run across the road, even though there were cars coming?

- your dog ran into the road and there was a car coming?

- you came home from school to find the front door open and things scattered all over the house?

- you get separated from your parents in a shop? In the park?

- you saw a flasher?

- you got an upsetting phone call in which someone said dirty words?

- you saw a syringe on the ground?

- a grownup or teenager asked you to keep a touch a secret?

- you were scared of the dark?

- you hated the babysitter but were frightened to tell your parents?

- a man and woman drive up in a lovely car and ask you for directions?

- your little sister/brother was being bullied by someone you knew?

- you and your brother were planning a surprise for your

Keeping Safe, © Michele Elliott 1985, 1986, 1988

mum's birthday and promised each other not to tell. Should you tell your mum?

- you were home alone and a delivery man came to the door with some groceries and asked to be let in? A person with a large bunch of flowers came? The milkman? The postman? Your cousin? Your sister?

- a stranger says your mum is ill and offers to take you home?

- your mum says you have to kiss someone goodbye, but you don't want to because you're shy or you just don't feel like it?

- you see a fire in your neighbour's house?

- you are alone and the telephone rings? The man wants to talk to your father?

- a person comes to the door and says there is an emergency? The person asks to use the telephone and you are at home alone?

- someone you know always tickles you and you hate it?

- you are in a wheelchair and people keep patting you on the head, even though you don't like it?

- you have to stay with a relative who makes you feel really uncomfortable? You have to try to explain to your mum?

- you had your bike stolen by a gang of bullies who warned you not to tell 'or else'?

- you are taking a short cut through the park, which your parents have told you not to do? A man follows/grabs you, says/does rude things and makes you promise not to tell. You know your parents will be angry because you shouldn't have gone into the park alone.

- friends of yours offer you some powder to swallow,

Keeping Safe, © Michele Elliott 1985, 1986, 1988

saying it will make you feel wonderful?

- a policeman comes to your door and asks to come in while you are on your own? (Police officers carry warrant cards and are obliged to produce them when asked. Although this verifies their identity, children should not let *anyone* in if they are alone.)

Keeping Safe, ©Michele Elliott 1985, 1986, 1988

'WHAT IF?' QUESTIONS TO ASK YOUR TEENS

What if . . .

- someone offered you drugs?

- you got on a bus and the person next to you started whispering obscenities to you?

- a bully made you pay them money every day?

- you were abducted and riding along in a car with your abductor?

- someone you met at a disco offered to take you home?

- a boy/girl you know wants to sleep with you? You know they have a reputation for sleeping around?

- you are being followed on a street late at night? There are houses, but no one seems to be up?

- you are being followed as you jog in the park?

- you are grabbed from behind by someone with a weapon?

- you find out a friend has AIDS and he/she is planning to sleep with another friend of yours who does not know?

- you receive an obscene telephone call when you are home alone? The caller says he can see you and threatens you?

Keeping Safe, © Michele Elliott 1985, 1986, 1988

- you are babysitting and the doorbell rings? You look through the peephole and see a delivery man with flowers?

- you are invited to a party when your friend's parents are out of town? You suspect the parents would be furious if they knew?

- a friend of yours was being abused and told you, but asked you not to tell anyone else?

- you are alone working in a shop when a robber comes in and demands the money in the till?

- you are on your paper round and a car starts following you slowly?

- you are babysitting and the person driving you home is drunk? It is very late and your parents are asleep at home?

- you see a stranger steal something from a shop?

- you see your best friend steal something from a shop?

- you are in a public toilet and the man next to you tries to molest you?

- you are babysitting and a small fire breaks out in the kitchen? The children are asleep upstairs.

- you get drunk at a party, but your parents don't know you are even at a party? You need to go home...

- you are offered a chance to see a pornographic video with some friends?

- you are in a video arcade when a man comes up to you and offers to pay for your games because he likes young people and has grandchildren your age?

- a friend of yours offered you some cocaine and urged you to try it just once? He says you're a coward if you don't and it is only an experiment.

Keeping Safe, © Michele Elliott 1985, 1986, 1988

- you are walking home from the bus when a man and woman in a car pull up to ask you for directions?

- a friend or relative of yours tries to touch you in a way you don't like?

- you find out your little brother is sniffing glue and he begs you not to tell?

- you are in a lift and the door is just closing when a person gets in who makes you feel very uncomfortable?

- a relative or friend of yours has a drinking problem?

- you feel suicidal?

- you think there is no one to talk to who would understand you?

- a friend confides that he/she is a drug addict? You're the only one who knows and you've promised to keep it a secret.

- your little sister tells you that she is being bullied at school and doesn't want to go any more?

- friends told you they were going out to get drunk and planned to drive home? You are invited, but sworn to secrecy.

- you came home alone to find the door to your flat open and heard the sound of things being broken?

- someone flashed at you?

- while you are in a place your parents have forbidden, you are assaulted, robbed, etc? You think your parents will be furious with you and never let you out again.

Keeping Safe, © Michele Elliott 1985, 1986, 1988

APPENDIX II

QUESTIONNAIRE FOR YOUNG TEENAGERS

This questionnaire is designed to be used as a tool for communicating with young people about keeping safe from assault. It is not meant to be a test which is marked, but a way of opening up the subject without being alarmist. You may not always agree with the answers; some could be true or false depending upon the circumstances. The answers are given as a guide.

The questionnaire does not mention sex abuse or rape, but does use the word assault. It can be used with younger or less mature teens. The questionnaire in Appendix III is for older teens.

QUESTIONS

1. You have the right to be safe. **T F**
2. You should always keep secrets if you promise not to tell. **T F**
3. A bribe is given to make you do something you do not want to do. **T F**
4. People are either good or bad. **T F**
5. Only bad people who look strange hurt children. **T F**
6. Adults do not always believe children. **T F**
7. Children should always obey adults. **T F**
8. You sometimes have the right to break rules. **T F**
9. It is a good idea to answer the telephone by repeating your name or your telephone number. **T F**
10. You should never lie. **T F**
11. You should never fight back if someone attacks you. **T F**
12. You have the right to tell anyone, even someone you know and trust, not to touch you in any way which makes you feel uncomfortable. **T F**
13. Jealousy is a sign of true love. **T F**

Keeping Safe, © Michele Elliott 1985, 1986, 1988

14. You should never hurt anyone's feelings. **T F**

15. Looking foolish in front of others is really embarrassing. **T F**

16. Boys are usually encouraged to be sensitive and gentle with girls. **T F**

17. When a child is assaulted, the offender is usually a stranger. **T F**

18. Girls are assaulted much more often than boys. **T F**

19. The vast majority of attackers are men. **T F**

20. The best way to escape a potential assault is to vomit. **T F**

21. A 'real man' shows the girl that he is the boss. **T F**

22. Generally the more attractive a girl is the greater her chance of being assaulted. **T F**

23. It is sometimes the victim's fault that he/she was assaulted. **T F**

24. People are much safer from assault at home. **T F**

25. If you or someone you know is assaulted, you should tell a trusted adult immediately. **T F**

Keeping Safe, © Michele Elliott 1985, 1986, 1988

ANSWERS

1. You have the right to be safe. **True**

2. You should always keep secrets if you promise not to tell. **False**
   Some secrets should not be kept. If anyone asks you to keep touching a secret or if you feel confused, uncomfortable or frightened by a secret, find a trusted adult to tell.

3. A bribe is given to make you do something you do not want to do. **True**

4. People are either good or bad. **False**

5. Only bad people who look strange hurt children. **False**

6. Adults do not always believe children. **True**
   If the first person you tell a problem to does not believe you, keep telling until someone does.

7. Children should always obey adults. **False**
   In order to keep safe, it may be necessary to disobey an adult.

8. You sometimes have the right to break rules. **True**
   To keep safe, you have the right to break any rules.

9. It is a good idea to answer the telephone

Keeping Safe, © Michele Elliott 1985, 1986, 1988

by repeating your name or your
telephone number. **False**

10. You should never lie. **False**
You might have to lie to keep safe. For example, you could say that your mum was waiting for you across the road if someone was bothering you.

11. You should never fight back if someone attacks you. **False**
If you feel in danger, you should do whatever you can to keep safe, such as kick, yell, bite, etc.

12. You have the right to tell anyone, even someone you know and trust, not to touch you in any way which makes you feel uncomfortable. **True**
You have the right to say who touches your body.

13. Jealousy is a sign of true love. **False**
Love depends upon mutual trust. Jealousy is based upon lack of trust.

14. You should never hurt anyone's feelings. **False**
In order to keep yourself safe, you may have to say no to someone you know and like, which might hurt his or her feelings.

15. Looking foolish in front of others is really embarrassing. **True**
But do not be afraid to look foolish if you feel inside that something is wrong. If you think you should leave a party, for example, because you do not like what is happening, do leave even if

Keeping Safe, © Michele Elliott 1985, 1986, 1988

you are embarrassed. It might keep you safe.

16. Boys are usually encouraged to be sensitive and gentle with girls. **False**
Girls should make it clear to boys that they like boys who are not afraid to be kind. Boys often think that girls only like the 'macho' type.

17. When a child is assaulted, the offender is usually a stranger. **False**
Over seventy-five per cent of people who assault children are known to the children.

18. Girls are assaulted much more often than boys. **False**
Boys are almost as much at risk as girls, though boys less often report an asasult.

19. The vast majority of assaults are committed by men. **True**
Over ninety per cent of reported assaults are committed by men. However, most men would never attack anyone.

20. The best way to escape a potential assault is to vomit. **False**
While it may work, conversations with offenders indicate that these kinds of tactics make them angry, rather than disgusted. Many people feel that an immediate spirited phsyical self-defence, including loud yelling, kicking, hitting, etc., is best because the element of surprise helps the victim to get away. Some people have

Keeping Safe, © Michele Elliott 1985, 1986, 1988

successfully talked their way out of dangerous situations. Each person must decide what is best according to the circumstances.

21. A 'real man' shows the girl that he is the boss. **False**
Why should one partner be boss?

22. Generally the more attractive a girl is the greater her chance of being assaulted. **False**
Studies have shown that being physically attractive has nothing to do with assault.

23. It is sometimes the victim's fault that he/she was assaulted. **False**
It is always the offender's fault. No one deserves to be assaulted.

24. People are much safer from assault at home. **False**
In a recent London survey, fifty-one per cent of assaults happened either in the victim's or the assailant's home.

25. If you or someone you know is assaulted, you should tell a trusted adult immediately. **True**
Think about people who would believe you and who would help you make a decision about what to do. An assault is too big a burden to carry in secret and getting help early will often lessen the trauma.

Keeping Safe, ©Michele Elliott 1985, 1986, 1988

APPENDIX III
QUESTIONNAIRE FOR OLDER TEENAGERS

One way to begin talking with young people about keeping safe from sexual abuse and assault is to give them this questionnaire or take it with them. It is not meant to be a quiz to be marked, but a basis for communication. Although answers are given, in some cases you may disagree with the answer. The desired outcome should be that teenagers think about and plan what to do should they be placed in a dangerous situation. This isn't a contest to get the 'right' answer.

This questionnaire does mention the terms sex abuse and rape and should be used with more mature teenagers.

QUESTIONS

1. You have the right to tell anyone, even someone you know and trust, not to touch you in any way which makes you feel uncomfortable. **T F**

2. When a girl says 'no' to a boy, she frequently means 'yes'. **T F**

3. A boy has a right to expect more than a kiss after he has spent money on a date. **T F**

4. Jealousy is a sign of true love. **T F**

5. Birth control is the female's responsibility. **T F**

6. Boys are not encouraged to be sensitive and gentle with girls. **T F**

7. Sexual frustration can be physically harmful. **T F**

8. People who fantasise about being seduced or raped have emotional problems. **T F**

9. Most date rapes occur because a girl teases a boy to the point that he cannot control himself. **T F**

10. Alcohol and/or drugs can lower inhibitions about engaging in sexual activity. **T F**

11. When a child is molested, the molester is usually a stranger. **T F**

Keeping Safe, ©Michele Elliott 1985, 1986, 1988

12. Girls are molested much more often than boys. **T F**

13. The vast majority of sexual abusers are men. **T F**

14. The best way to escape a potential rapist is to vomit. **T F**

15. A 'real man' shows the girl that he is the boss. **T F**

16. Generally the more attractive a girl is the higher her chance of being sexually assaulted. **T F**

17. When a girl is sexually assaulted, she usually has done something to provoke it. **T F**

18. It is against the law for a boy to engage in sexual intercouse with a girl under sixteen, even with her consent. **T F**

19. Sexual gratification is the major reason for rape. **T F**

20. Males who are sexually assaulted suffer the same kind of emotional trauma as female victims. **T F**

21. People are much safer from sexual assault at home. **T F**

22. Less than half of all rapes are reported to the police. **T F**

23. An assailant rarely finds it necessary to use a weapon to commit rape. **T F**

24. People who sexually assault others are psychologically disturbed. **T F**

Keeping Safe, © Michele Elliott 1985, 1986, 1988

25. Rapists are secret, solitary offenders who usually attack their victims when the rapist is alone. **T F**

26. Teenage and adult victims of sexual assault seldom know the identity of the offender. **T F**

27. Sexual assault is usually an unplanned, spontaneous act. **T F**

28. There are many false reports of rape by women seeking revenge on their boyfriends. **T F**

29. If female victim feels uncomfortable talking with a male police officer, she has the right to request that a female officer be called. **T F**

30. Since the rape victim is often unprotected by contraceptives, she will probably become pregnant. **T F**

31. The victim is allowed to have a friend stay with her during the medical examination or questioning. **T F**

32. During an investigation of a rape, the victim can refuse to answer questions irrelevant to the rape. **T F**

33. If a woman is raped, her name will be published by the media reporting her case. **T F**

34. As a rule, the rape victim can be asked questions in court about her sexual conduct. **T F**

35. If you or someone you know has been sexually assaulted, you should tell a trusted adult immediately. **T F**

Keeping Safe, © Michele Elliott 1985, 1986, 1988

ANSWERS

1. You have the right to tell anyone, even someone you know and trust, not to touch you in any way which makes you feel uncomfortable. **True**
   Since a high percentage of the assaults on teenagers are by an adult known to them, it is important to learn to say no not only to strangers, but to friends, family members or acquaintances.

2. When a girl says 'no' to a boy, she frequently means 'yes'. **False**
   This attitude is left over from old films and books. Boys and girls should discuss together their ideas about mixed messages so that both understand the expectations and the misconceptions of the other.

3. A boy has a right to expect more than a kiss after he has spent money on a date. **False**
   If this is his attitude, 'go Dutch'.

4. Jealousy is a sign of true love. **False**
   Love depends upon mutual trust. Jealousy is based upon lack of trust.

5. Birth control is the female's responsibility. **False**
   It should be a shared responsibility.

Keeping Safe, © Michele Elliott 1985, 1986, 1988

6. Boys are not encouraged to be sensitive and gentle with girls. **True**
   Most boys are raised to believe that being tough and macho is what girls expect of them. This should be discussed so that girls and boys can decide what they value in a relationship.

7. Sexual frustration can be physically harmful. **False**
   Boys have used this line for years!

8. People who fantasise about being seduced or raped have emotional problems. **False**
   Some people have 'seduction' fantasies. In the fantasy, they are in control; they choose the 'assailant', place, circumstances, etc. The reality of rape is different – violent and sadistic.

9. Most date rapes occur because a girl teases the boy to the point that he cannot control himself. **False**
   This attitude blames the victim. Rape occurs because the assailant has problems with anger, aggression, hostility and power.

10. Alcohol and/or drugs can lower inhibitions about engaging in sexual activity. **True**
    Studies have shown this to be true for both sexes.

11. When a child is molested, the molester is usually a stranger. **False**
    The child knows the attacker in at least seventy-five per cent of the reported cases of child molestation.

Keeping Safe, ©Michele Elliott 1985, 1986, 1988

12. Girls are molested much more often than boys. **False**
    Statistics vary, but boys are almost as much at risk as girls. The victimisation of boys is reported less often, partly because of the fear of being branded as a homosexual after an attack.

13. The vast majority of sexual abusers are men. **True**
    Ninety per cent of reported attacks were committed by men.

14. The best way to escape a potential rapist is to vomit. **False**
    While it may work, conversations with convicted rapists indicate that these kinds of tactics make them angry, rather than disgusted. Many people feel that an immediate spirited physical defence, including loud yelling, kicking, hitting, etc. is best because the element of surprise would help the victim to get away. Some people have successfully talked their way out of rape, but each must decide for herself according to the circumstances.

15. A 'real man' shows the girl that he is the boss. **False**
    Why should one partner be the boss? This implies that the girl is incapable of directing her own life. It places her in the same category as a docile pet.

16. Generally the more attractive a girl is the higher her chance of being sexually assaulted. **False**
    Studies of assault victims have shown

Keeping Safe, © Michele Elliott 1985, 1986, 1988

that being physically attractive has nothing to do with sexual assault.

7. When a girl is sexually assaulted, she usually has done something to provoke it. **False**
In the United States, the National Commission on the Causes and Prevention of Violence did a study on crimes of violence and paid particular attention to the role of the victim in cases of murder, assault, robbery and rape. The commission wanted to determine whether victims of these crimes in any way provoked them or rashly touched off the action against them. It was discovered that victims of rape were responsible for less provocative behaviour or unwitting collusion than victims of murder, assault or robbery. The cases on file of the rape of individuals of all ages, from three-month-old babies to ninety-seven-year-old women, show how ridiculous this myth really is.

8. It is against the law for a boy to engage in sexual intercouse with a girl under sixteen, even with her consent. **True**
The legal age of consent is sixteen.

9. Sexual gratification is the major reason for rape. **False**
Rape is about violence, not sex. If you hit someone over the head with your rolling pin, it is not called cooking.

20. Males who are sexually assaulted suffer the same kind of emotional trauma as female victims. **True**

eeping Safe, ©Michele Elliott 1985, 1986, 1988

Sexual assault on males is reported even less often than assault on females and there is no support system, such as Rape Crisis Centres, for male victims.

21. People are much safer from sexual assault at home. **False**
In a recent London survey (see p 175), fifty-one per cent of sexual assaults happened either in the victim's or the assailant's home.

22. Less than half of all rapes are reported to the police. **True**
Only one in twelve are reported, according to the London survey.

23. An assailant rarely finds it necessary to use a weapon to commit rape. **True**
Only a small proportion of sexual assaults involve weapons. Most assailants use superior size and fear to subdue victims.

24. People who sexually assault others are psychologically disturbed. **False**
Most test as 'normal' on psychological tests.

25. Rapists are secret, solitary offenders who usually attack their victims when the rapist is alone. **True**
In only one in a hundred cases in the London survey was there more than one assailant.

26. Teenage and adult victims seldom know the identity of the rapist. **False**
Over sixty per cent of attacks in the

Keeping Safe, © Michele Elliott 1985, 1986, 1988

London survey were known to the victim.

27. Sexual assault is usually an unplanned, spontaneous act. **False**
Most sexual assaults are planned.

28. There are many false reports of rape by women seeking revenge on their boyfriends. **False**
In a study in New York of all the reported rapes in one year, only two per cent turned out to be false.

29. If a female victim feels uncomfortable talking with a male police officer, she has the right to request that a female officer be called. **True**
While a victim has the right to request this, the police have no obligation to provide a female officer. The police do try to comply with this request, if at all possible.

30. Since the rape victim is often unprotected by contraceptives, she will probably become pregnant. **False**
Only a small percentage of rape victims become pregnant.

31. The victim is allowed to have a friend stay with her during the medical examination or questioning. **True**
This can be a family member or close friend.

32. During an investigation of a rape, the victim can refuse to answer questions irrelevant to the rape. **True**
Questions about a victim's personal

Keeping Safe, ©Michele Elliott 1985, 1986, 1988

life, not relevant to the rape, need
not be answered.

33. If a woman is raped, her name will be
published by the media reporting her
case. **False**
**Rape victims are entitled to anonymity
before, during and after the trial.**

34. As a rule, the rape victim can be asked
questions in court about her sexual
conduct. **False**
**In court a rape victim may not be
asked questions about her previous
sexual conduct unless the judge is
satisfied that these questions are
relevant to the defence.**

35. If you or someone you know has been
sexually assaulted, you should tell a
trusted adult immediately. **True**
**Think about the people who would
believe you and who would help you in
making a decision about what to do.
Sexual assault is too big a burden to
carry in secret and getting supportive
help early will often lessen the trauma.
If you feel completely alone, telephone
the local Rape Crisis Centre (the number
is in the directory) or telephone the
London office on (01) 837 1600 for
information. If the offender is an adult
who is known to the child or a family
member, contact the Incest Crisis line
on (01) 890 4732 or (01) 422 5100.
ChildLine, on 0800 1111, is a 24 hour
telephone service for children or
teenagers in distress.**

Keeping Safe, © Michele Elliott 1985, 1986, 1988

APPENDIX IV
SOURCES OF INFORMATION

CHILDRENS BOOKS

TITLE: **The Anti-Colouring Book** (ages 4 up)
AUTHOR: Susan Striker and Edward Kimmel
ISBN: 0-590-70011-1
PUBLISHER: Scholastic

This is one of a series of excellent books designed to enhance children's creativity and ability to express their feelings. Can be used as a follow up to prevention programmes, to help children who have been abused or just to give to kids for the fun of it.

TITLE: **The Body Book** (ages 4 to 11)
AUTHOR: Claire Rayner
ISBN: 0-330-25807-9
PUBLISHER: Piccolo Books

Brilliantly simple explanations of how the body works, from breathing, to bleeding to tasting, seeing, hearing, making babies and growing old and dying, this book has it all. Clear, friendly language and illustrations make this a delight to use with children. A video of the book available from Video Arts.

TITLE: **The Getting Better Book** (ages 4 to 11)
AUTHOR: Claire Rayner
ISBN: 0-330-29358-3
PUBLISHER: Piccolo Books

When children ask why questions about being sick, germs, 'scratches, wallops and bumps', or going to hospital, this book will give you the right words to help them understand. Wonderfully illustrated by Tony King.

TITLE: **Boy** (ages 8 to adult)
AUTHOR: Roald Dahl
ISBN: 0-14-008917-9
PUBLISHER: Penguin

Into his description of a charmed childhood spent in Wales and Norway, the author weaves the story of the cruel and barbaric treatment he received at an English public school. Compulsive reading, as you would expect from Roald Dahl.

TITLE: **Bruce's Story** (ages 3 to 7)
AUTHORS: M. Thom and C. Macliver
ISBN: 0-907324-27-4
PUBLISHER: Children's Society

Bruce is a dog who talks about having to leave his mum and dad to live in a kennel with his brothers and sisters. He watches them go to a new home and eventually finds himself with a new family. Designed for children who are fostered, adopted or taken into care.

TITLE: **Come and Tell Me** (ages 3 to 6)
AUTHOR: Helen Hollick
ISBN: 0-85122-660-4
PUBLISHER: Dinosaur

Small colour picture book for young children warning them about the dangers of going off without telling their parents and of going off with strangers. Lots of good hugging pictures, but Jenny should not have been shown talking to a stranger. The author's approach is very positive and low-key; children will not be frightened by this one.

TITLE: **Got To Be Me** (ages 5 to 10)
AUTHOR: Merrill Harmin
ISBN: 0-913592-80-3
PUBLISHER: Argus

A book for children to fill in with stories. For example, children finish the sentence, 'I like to pretend I...' or 'If I have my own children someday, I'll be sure to...' Useful for getting children to talk about feelings and ideas.

TITLE: **No More Secrets for Me** (ages 4 to 8)
AUTHOR: O. Wachter
ISBN: 0-14-009287-0
PUBLISHER: Penguin (Viking Kest hardcover)

Adapted from an American book of the same name, this contains four stories of children being approached in a frightening, confusing or sexually inappropriate way by adults, including a female babysitter; a female and male stranger team; a male camp counsellor shown in a tent with a boy, both of them nude; and a stepfather touching his stepdaughter under her nightdress. Should be used with care.

TITLE: **There's a Nightmare in My Cupboard** (ages 3 to 7)
AUTHOR: Mercer Mayer
ISBN: 0-907144-33-0
PUBLISHER: Methuen Moonlight

Charming little colour picture book showing the nightmare as a monster which is eventually tamed by the child. Useful to help any children talk about their fears and worries.

TITLE: **This is Me** (ages 7 to 9)
AUTHOR: Merrill Harmin
ISBN: 0-89505-019-6
PUBLISHER: Argus

A fill-in book for children to help them to discuss feelings by completing sentences such as, 'I would not want to be...' or 'Suppose I were feeling lonely, I might feel OK about reaching out to someone if...'

TITLE: **We Can Say No** (ages 3 to 6)
AUTHORS: D Pithers and Sarah Green
ISBN: 0-09-950690-4
PUBLISHER: Beaver Books

Nicely illustrated colour picture book to be read aloud to young children. Designed to help children think about ways to get out of potentially dangerous situations.

TITLE: **Willow Street Kids** (ages 7 to 11)
AUTHOR: Michele Elliott
ISBN: 0-233-97954-9
PUBLISHER: MME/Andre Deutsch & Pan

Based upon the true stories of children, this book has been written in an entertaining way to help children figure out what to do in a variety of situations, from bullying to getting lost, to unwelcome advances from adults, known and unknown. It has been used in schools and at home with enthusiastic responses from children, parents and teachers. Low-key, non-explicit.

ADULT BOOKS

TITLE: **The ABC of Child Abuse Work**
AUTHOR: Jean Moore
ISBN: 0-566-00860-2
PUBLISHER: Gower

Practical guide for professionals and students on qualifying courses. The emphasis is on the child's perspective. The book includes case illustrations and methods of working directly with abused and neglected children. There is also a model for working with parents, as well as analysis of the reasons for child abuse.

TITLE: **Ask Any Woman: A London inquiry into rape and sexual assault**
AUTHOR: Ruth E. Hall
ISBN: 0-90504-628-5
PUBLISHER: Falling Wall Press

Based upon a self-selecting survey of women in London, it relates their experiences of being raped and of being victims of child sexual abuse.

TITLE: **Child Abuse: The Developing Child**
AUTHORS: Ruth S. Kempe and C. Henry Kempe
ISBN: 0-00-686120-2
PUBLISHER: Fontana Books

Clearly written and comprehensive guide to understanding child abuse. Written by the acknowledged experts in the field, this book is essential for any library on child abuse.

TITLE: **Child Sexual Abuse Within the Family**
AUTHOR: Ruth Porter (ed)
ISBN: 0-442-79290-X
PUBLISHER: Tavistock

Provides guidance on the actions to be taken by professionals involved in the management of sexual abuse cases within the family. This book was the first of its kind in the United Kingdom.

TITLE: **The Common Secret: Sexual Abuse of Children**
AUTHORS: Ruth S. Kempe and C. Henry Kempe
ISBN: 0-7167-1625-9
PUBLISHER: Freeman

From the respected pioneers in the field of child abuse, this practical, comprehensive resource gives an insightful look into child sexual abuse, from paedophilia and exhibition, to rape and child pornography. The Kempes allay many of the myths which have hindered a fair appraisal of the problem's severity during the past twenty-five years. Includes details of the Incest Diversion Programme for incestuous fathers.

TITLE: **Cry Hard and Swim**
AUTHOR: Jacqueline Spring
ISBN: 0-86068-813-5
PUBLISHER: Virago

In letters to her mother, poems and narrative, the painful story of father-daughter incest emerges. Through therapy and hard work, Jacqueline heals herself and helps others.

TITLE: **A Crying Game: The Diary of a Battered Wife**
AUTHOR: Janine Turner
ISBN: 0-906391-52-0
PUBLISHER: Mainstream Publishing

The author uses her diary of everyday events to describe in vivid detail how she became a battered wife, how she regained her self-respect and helped others. Very useful for anyone who wonders how this kind of violence happens.

TITLE: **Demon Drink**
AUTHOR: Jancis Robinson
ISBN: 0-855-33692-7
PUBLISHER: Mitchell Beazley

Thoroughly researched and practical in approach, this book charts the effects of alcohol on mental and physical health.

TITLE: **For Your Own Good: The Roots of Violence in Child Rearing**
AUTHOR: Alice Miller
ISBN: 0-860-68899-2
PUBLISHER: Virago

Explores attitudes that emphasise discipline and obedience and the links to such authoritarians as Hitler (he was abused as a child).

TITLE: **Handbook of Clinical Intervention in Child Sexual Abuse**
AUTHOR: Suzanne M Sgroi, MD
ISBN: 0-669-05213-2
PUBLISHER: Lexington Books

Drawing on years of intensive work with cases of sexual abuse, Sgroi sets forth a model of active, coordinated intervention within the family which offers help for the victim. She stresses joint working of the professionals and how to provide a network. This invaluable book presents step-by-step procedures for reporting, investigating and validating the offence; interviewing the child and preparing for court. Although American based, the vast majority of the information is useful and valid for the United Kingdom.

TITLE: **Love and Pain: A Survival Handbook for Women**
AUTHOR: Sandra Horley
ISBN: 0-7199-1214-8
PUBLISHER: Bedford Square Press

By the director of Chiswick Family Rescue, this guide gives advice and information to help women deal with abusive situations.

TITLE: **Men Who Rape: The Psychology of the Offender**
AUTHOR: A. Nicholas Groth
ISBN: 0-306-40268-8
PUBLISHER: Plenum Publishing Company

Easily read non-technical book which provides a framework for understanding the histories of abusers, their motivations and how it is possible to treat them.

TITLE: **Solvent Abuse: The Adolescent Epidemic?**
AUTHOR: Dr. Joyce Watson
ISBN: 0-7099-3684-2
PUBLISHER: Croom Helm

Examines the factors involved in solvent abuse, the experiences and views of parents, treatment responses, and community action. It is drawn from research done by the author in the Strathclyde region.

TITLE: **Thou Shalt Not Be Aware: Society's Betrayal of the Child**
AUTHOR: A. Miller
ISBN: 0-7453-0049-9
PUBLISHER: Pluto Press

The author attacks the popular myth of infantile sexuality and shows how it is normally an excuse for the exploitation of children. She uses case histories and describes with devastating directness the effects in adulthood of early traumas.

Parents Books

TITLE: **Anorexia Nervosa: A Guide for Sufferers and Their Families**
AUTHOR: R. L. Palmer
ISBN: 0-14-022065-8
PUBLISHER: Penguin

Discusses the causes, symptoms and treatment of anorexia in light of current medical opinion. The author gives practical suggestions for families and anorexics.

TITLE: **The Art of Starvation: An Adolescence Observed**
AUTHOR: Sheila Macleod
ISBN: 0-86068-169-6
PUBLISHER: Virago

This is the personal story of how the author came to terms with anorexia. Based upon her diaries, it is a remarkable account of the underlying issues in this illness.

TITLE: **Brief Lives**
AUTHOR: Suzanne Foster and Pamela Smith
ISBN: 0-85140-706-4
PUBLISHER: Arlington Books/Thames Television

Relates the experiences of families who have lost children through illness, accident, murder or suicide. Explores ways to help parents cope and includes a list of helpful organisations and publications.

TITLE: **Children, Parents and the Law**
AUTHOR: E. Rudinger
ISBN: 0-340-37256-7
PUBLISHER: Consumers' Association

Very useful and practical book for anyone dealing with questions about the rights of parents and children in legal situations. It is clear, concise and lists many referral agencies for further information.

TITLE: **Drug Warning**
AUTHOR: D. Stockley
ISBN: 0-356-12424-X
PUBLISHER: Macdonald

An illustrated guide designed especially to help parents and teachers recognise the various kinds of drugs, as well as the signs and symptoms of drug abuse.

TITLE: **It's OK to Say No** (ages 4 to 7)
AUTHOR: R. Lenett
ISBN: 0-7225-1328-3
PUBLISHER: Thorsons

A read-aloud-together-book, this has been adapted from an American edition. Some good information, though saying that 'in effect children must learn to be distrustful of adults...' and other similar statements are a bit scare-mongering.

TITLE: **The Safe Child Book**
AUTHOR: Sherryll Kerns Kraiser
ISBN: 0-7088-3036-6
PUBLISHER: Futura

Contains much practical advice for keeping children safe from an American expert in the field. The contact numbers are based in the States.

TEENS BOOKS

TITLE: **Children and The Law**
AUTHOR: Maggie Rae
ISBN: 0-582-89334-8
PUBLISHER: Longman

Clearly explains to young people what their rights are under the law. Because of the way it is presented, it is also a valuable guide for anyone dealing with young people.

TITLE: **Push Me, Pull Me**
AUTHOR: Sandra Chick
ISBN: 0-7043-4901-9
PUBLISHER: Women's Press 'Livewire'

A fourteen-year-old girl's world collapses when her mum's boyfriend moves in and sexually assaults her. When he leaves and she tells, the process of healing starts. Winner of the Other Award, 1987.

TITLE: **Safe, Strong, and Streetwise**
AUTHOR: Helen Benedict
ISBN: 0-340-48495-0
PUBLISHER: Hodder and Stoughton

This contains a massive amount of information and is especially useful as a reference resource for schools and parents, as well as for teens themselves.

TITLE: **Too Close Encounters and What To Do About Them**
AUTHOR: Rosemary Stones
ISBN: 0-946826-69-2
PUBLISHER: Piccadilly Press

Based upon common sense and practical strategies for dealing with everything from flashers to rape, this guide is full of valuable ideas for young people. It includes a good resource list at the end for obtaining further help and information.

FICTION

TITLE: **Back in the First Person** (teens and up)
AUTHOR: Kathy Page
ISBN: 0-86068-642-6
PUBLISHER: Virago

The rape of Cath by her former boyfriend leads to a painful year of self-examination and the traumas of going to court. Eventually Cath moves back into control of her own life. Helpful to young people who have been raped and to others to understand the far-reaching consequences of this kind of violence.

TITLE: **Don't Tell Your Mother** (teens and up)
AUTHOR: T. Hart
ISBN: 0-7043-33772-4
PUBLISHER: Quartet Books

The behaviour and emotions of Shirley and her parents are looked at in depth in this novel about incest. The ending illustrates how the attitudes of society can destroy rather than help. Can be upsetting, but especially useful for exploring the issues with young people.

TITLE: **If I Should Die Before I Wake** (adults)
AUTHOR: Michele Morris
ISBN: 0-285-62575-6
PUBLISHER: Souvenir Press

In one of the most powerful books ever written about father-daughter incest, Michelle Morris has captured the horror of Carla's life in a vivid and compelling style which makes it impossible to put down the novel until the last page.

TITLE: **Porky** (teens and up)
AUTHOR: D. Moggach
ISBN: 0-14-006943-7
PUBLISHER: Penguin Books

A story of incest between father and daughter told with great compassion. Can be used with teens, but should be read by the adult before doing so.

PERSONAL STORIES

TITLE: **I Know Why the Caged Bird Sings**
AUTHOR: M. Angelou
ISBN: 0-86068-511-X
PUBLISHER: Virago

In this first volume of her autobiography, the author tells about her childhood in the American South of the 1930s. A visit to her mother ends with young Maya being raped by her mother's lover. Through her own inner strength, Maya overcomes this horrific event, goes on to discover the pleasures of dance and drama and gives birth to a much loved son.

TITLE: **I Never Told Anyone**
AUTHORS: E. Bass and L. Thornton
ISBN: 0-06-091050-X
PUBLISHER: Harper Colophon Books

Very moving collection of personal accounts of child sexual abuse written by women of all ages about the abuse they suffered as young girls or teenagers. Introduced by brief biographies that place each woman in a past and present context, the stories reflect a wide diversity of experience and emotional response.

GAMES

TITLE: **No Go Tell** (ages 5 to 11)
PUBLISHER: Selnec Products
PRICE: £19.80

Designed by a social worker to help protect children from sexual abuse, this game is bright and easy to play. Because the board is on a large poster format, it can be put up in the classroom for reference.

TITLE: **Safe and Smart** (ages 5 to 11)
PUBLISHER: Parker Games
PRICE: £8.99

Four games for children around the themes of using the telephone, safety in the home, finding your way safely to the shops and home, and bicycle safety. Designed for two to four players, it is a good resource for parents.

TITLE: **Safely Home** (ages 5 to 11)
PUBLISHER: Parker Games
PRICE: £11.00

Designed to be used at home or in the classroom, this game rewards the one who gets home safely, not necessarily first. Tokens are given for sensible answers and actions and the one with the most tokens wins. Kidscape helped to design this and it has been very well reviewed. Children enjoy playing it.

LEAFLETS

TITLE: **Being a Proper Stranger**
PUBLISHER: National Children's Home
ADDRESS: 85c Highbury Park, London N5 1UD
PRICE: Free

Foldover leaflet giving advice to adults about what to do and how to behave with children they don't know.

TITLE: **How to Help Them Stay Safe**
PUBLISHER: Kidscape
ADDRESS: 82 Brook Street, London W1Y 1YG
PRICE: Free with large SAE

Sixteen page guide for parents to help them talk with their children about bullies, strangers and known adults who may try to harm them. It talks about how to keep safe from sexual abuse without using the term 'sexual abuse' with children. The first one available in the UK, it includes Points for Parents, the Kidscape Keepsafe Code for children, possible Danger Signs, What to do if your child tells you about abuse, and Where to go for help and advice.

TITLE: **If in Doubt, Shout**
PUBLISHER: ChildWatch
ADDRESS: 60 Beck Road, Everthrope, Brough, Humberside
PRICE: £0.50

ChildWatch has a large folder of information available from various sources, including their own. The fifty pence covers posting.

TITLE: **Keeping Your Children Out of Danger**
PUBLISHER: National Children's Home
ADDRESS: 85c Highbury Park, London N5 1UD
PRICE: Free

Foldover leaflet giving ideas for dealing with children, such as listening to them and giving them attention.

TITLE: **Protect Your Child**
PUBLISHER: NSPCC
ADDRESS: 67 Saffron Hill, London EC1N 8RS
PRICE: Free

This guide answers sixteen questions about the sexual abuse of children, such as what to do if a parent suspects a partner of abusing a child, will a child who is abused be taken away from the parents and what to do if someone feels wrongly accused of child abuse.

PACKAGE FOR PROFESSIONALS

TITLE: **Self Esteem and Personal Safety**
AUTHOR: Eileen Vizard
PUBLISHER: Tavistock Publications

This video package is designed for professionals working in therapeutic situations with abused children. The video shows children learning to become assertive after they have been abused. Because the children really are abuse victims, this film needs to be used in a confidential manner. The work is based upon the author's experience of working with abused children at Great Ormond Street Hospital.

SCHOOL SAFETY PROGRAMMES

TITLE: **Kidscape Primary Kit**
AUTHOR: Michele Elliott
PUBLISHER: Kidscape

Prevention programme for five- to eleven-year-olds which deals with bullies, getting lost, strangers and threats from known adults. Includes a video for adults, five manuals, two hundred leaflets and one hundred posters. Available from Kidscape.

TITLE: **Kidscape Under Fives Manual**
AUTHOR: Michele Elliott
PUBLISHER: Kidscape

This manual is used with the Kidscape Primary Kit and provides the lesson plans for children aged three to five. It is also appropriate for some special needs children.

TALKING BOOKS FOR THE BLIND

TITLE: **Preventing Child Sexual Assault**
AUTHOR: Michele Elliott
CATALOGUE
NUMBER: T5548/2 cassettes

Practical advice about talking with children. Available from Customer Services, the Royal National Institute for the Blind, Braille House, 338-46 Goswell Road, London EC1V 7JE. Telephone: (01) 837 9921.

VIDEOS FOR CHILDREN

There has been a flood of 'prevention' videos into Britain, the vast majority of which have come from Canada and the States. The videos are intended to make children confident enough to deal with the possibility that someone might try to touch them in an inappropriate way. We feel there is no substitute for talking with children and we are concerned about the use of videos as a way to **introduce** sensitive subjects. However, some may be useful for follow-up work and reinforcing messages.

'Better Safe Than Sorry', 1, 2 & 3, Educational Media International, 25 Boileau Road, London W5 3AL. The presenter and group of child actors go through a series of 'keeping safe' situations. Seems false and staged. 14 minutes.

'Feeling Yes, Feeling No', Educational Media International, 25 Boileau Road, London W5 3AL. From the Canadian Film Board, this has three adults roleplaying possible sexually abusive situations in front of children in a classroom scene. The adults' portrayal of children is unrealistic and patronising. It uses the correct terminology, not slang, for parts of the body. 35 minutes.

'Have Fun – Take Care', Community Involvement Team, Tooting Police Station.
A video package with notes and props to assist police officers in the presentation to children of the subject of strangers. 20 minutes.

'Kids Can Say No', Skippon Video Associates Ltd, 43 Drury Lane, WC2. Rolf Harris talks to children and takes child actors through four situations. Uses same song as 'Feeling Yes, Feeling No'. The last scene could worry children who have not been abused. It could be quite useful as the basis for professional discussions. 20 minutes.

'No More Secrets', Educational Media International, 25 Boileau Road, London W5 3AL. Made by a Californian video company. Complicated messages which combine children talking with impressionistic cartoon drawings of sexually abusive situations. 13 minutes.

'Now I Can Tell You My Secret', Walt Disney Educational Services, 31–32 Soho Square, London W1V 6AP. This video has a continuous story line told from a child's viewpoint. The children do not seem to be acting and the story readily engages the attention of children. It is one of the best available. 15 minutes.

'Say No To Strangers', Home Office Film. Shown by the police in schools on request. 18 minutes.

'Stranger Danger', Thames Valley Police. Designed to illustrate to children the possible dangers there may be in public areas from people who are strangers. Uses Pippin, the dog, who helps save the child. 12 minutes.

'Strong Kids, Safe Kids', CIC Video, UIP House, 45 Beadon Road, Hammersmith, London W6. Using the Fonz and cartoon characters, this video attempts to reach adults and children through songs, gimmicks and frequent Hollywood-type message changes. It is long, confusing and open to misinterpretation by children and adults. 38 minutes.

'Time to Talk', The Samaritans. Designed to help young people to be better equipped to face and cope with crises and to show them how to find someone who has time to talk. Very good, as we've come to expect from The Samaritans. 20 minutes.

VIDEOS FOR ADULTS

'Adam', Michael Tuchner. Odyssey, CBS Fox Video Ltd. The true story of the abduction and murder in Florida of the six-year-old only child of John and Rene Walsh. After a difficult struggle to maintain their sanity, they eventually succeed in forcing new legislation – The Missing Children Act. 'Adam' is a powerful film, difficult to watch, but well done. 92 minutes.

'Breaking Silence', Theresa Tollini/Future Education Films. Albany Videos, The Albany, Douglas Way, London SE8 4AG. An effective American film explaining the difficulties experienced by adult survivors of child sexual abuse. Given the strong emotions it evokes, careful preparations for support should always be made before showing it. 58 minutes.

'Child Molestation – Breaking the Silence', Walt Disney Educational Services, 31–32 Soho Square, London W1V 6AP. A talk for adults about the problem and statistics of child sexual assault, based upon the experience in the States. The laws and procedures mentioned are only applicable to the States. 20 minutes.

'Secret Sounds Screaming: The Sexual Abuse of Children', Ayoka Chenzira. Albany Videos, The Albany, Douglas Way, London SE8 4AG. This American film relies upon over-dramatised and strong emotional badgering which only serves to get in the way of its message. Using quick, disjointed segments from interviews which are meant to provoke and engage, it merely creates anger and confusion. 25 minutes.

'Sexual Abuse of Children', Film Unit, University of Leeds. Three videos intended to provide medical students with a background for child sexual abuse. 90 minutes.

'Talking with Sexually Abused Children', University of Leeds. Three videos for those working with children about practical ways to interview and help children. 90 minutes.

'Through the Eyes of a Child', Florence Hallum Prevention of Child Abuse Fund (UK), 36–38 Peckham Road, London SE5 8QR. Introduced by Michael Caine, this film looks at a group of adults (actors) in group 'therapy' who are discussing being sexually, physically and emotionally abused as children. Vivid flashbacks portray their fear as children. Includes a father who has beaten his son. 30 minutes.

APPENDIX V
SIGNS OF ABUSE

The following is an extract from the Kidscape Primary Kit:

It is important to note that these lists are only possible indicators of abuse. Many of the signs could have other explanations.

Some of the characteristic signs of abuse are the same, so there will be duplications in the lists provided. Although these signs do not necessarily indicate that a child has been abused, they may help adults recognise that something is wrong. The possibility of abuse should be investigated if a child shows one or more of these symptoms, or any one of them to a marked degree.

1. SIGNS OF PHYSICAL ABUSE

- unexplained injuries or burns, particularly if they are recurrent
- improbable excuses given to explain injuries
- refusal to discuss injuries
- untreated injuries
- admission of punishment which appears excessive
- fear of parents being contacted

- bald patches
- withdrawal from physical contact
- arms and legs kept covered in hot weather
- fear of returning home
- fear of medical help
- self-destructive tendencies
- aggression toward others
- running away

2. SIGNS OF EMOTIONAL ABUSE

- physical, mental and emotional development lags
- admission of punishment which appears excessive
- over-reaction to mistakes
- continual self-deprecation
- sudden speech disorders
- fear of new situations
- inappropriate emotional responses to painful situations
- neurotic behaviour (e.g. rocking; hair-twisting; thumb-sucking)
- self-mutilation
- fear of parents being contacted
- extremes of passivity or aggression
- drug/solvent abuse
- running away
- compulsive stealing; scavenging

3. NEGLECT

- constant hunger
- poor personal hygiene
- constant tiredness
- poor state of clothing
- emaciation
- frequent lateness or non-attendance at school
- untreated medical problems
- destructive tendencies
- low self-esteem
- neurotic behaviour (see 2)
- no social relationships
- running away
- compulsive stealing or scavenging

The different kinds of abuse can also be interrelated: a sexually abused child may be emotionally abused and neglected or physically abused as well. Almost by definition any child who has been physically or sexually abused or neglected has also been emotionally abused.

MORE NON-FICTION AVAILABLE FROM HODDER AND STOUGHTON PAPERBACKS

ELIZABETH WARD
☐ 42595 9　Timbo: A Struggle for Survival　　　　£2.99

All these books are available at your local bookshop or newsagent, or can be ordered direct from the publisher. Just tick the titles you want and fill in the form below.

Prices and availability subject to change without notice.

Hodder & Stoughton Paperbacks, P.O. Box 11, Falmouth, Cornwall.

Please send cheque or postal order for the value of the book, and add the following for postage and packing:

U.K. including B.F.P.O. £1.00 for one book, plus 50p for the second book, and 30p for each additional book ordered up to a £3.00 maximum.

OVERSEAS INCLUDING EIRE – £2.00 for the first book, plus £1.00 for the second book, and 50p for each additional book ordered.

OR Please debit this amount from my Access/Visa Card (delete as appropriate).

Card Number ☐☐☐☐☐☐☐☐☐☐☐☐☐☐☐☐☐☐

Amount £ ....

Expiry Date ....

Signed ....

Name ....

Address ....